STAFF AND
EDUCATIONAL
DEVELOPMENT

STAFF AND EDUCATIONAL DEVELOPMENT

CASE STUDIES, EXPERIENCE AND PRACTICE FROM HIGHER EDUCATION

EDITED BY

HELEN EDWARDS, DAVID BAUME & GRAHAM WEBB

CASE STUDIES OF TEACHING IN HIGHER EDUCATION

KOGAN
PAGE

LONDON AND STERLING, VA

First published in Great Britain and the United States in 2003 by Kogan Page Limited

120 Pentonville Road
London N1 9JN
UK
www.kogan-page.co.uk

22883 Quicksilver Drive
Sterling VA 20166-2012
USA

ISBN   0 7494 4021 X (paperback)
       0 7494 4061 9 (hardback)

British Library Cataloguing-in-Publication Data

A CIP record for this book is available from the British Library.

Library of Congress Cataloging-in-Publication Data

Staff and educational development : case studies, experience, and practice / edited by Helen Edwards, David Baume, and Graham Webb.
    p. cm.
Includes bibliographical references and index.
  ISBN 0-7494-4021-X (pbk.) -- ISBN 0-7494-4061-9 (hard)
  1. College teachers--In-service training--Case studies. 2. Career development--Case studies. 3. College personnel management--Case studies. I. Edwards, Helen, Ph.D. II. Baume, David, 1943- III. Webb, Graham, 1950-
  LB1738.S723 2003
  378.1'2'00715--dc21
                        2003011262

Typeset by Saxon Graphics Ltd, Derby
Printed and bound in Great Britain by Clays Ltd, St Ives plc

CONTENTS

CONTRIBUTORS

David Baume is a higher education consultant. He was founding chair of the UK Staff and Educational Development Association (SEDA) and is co-editor of the *International Journal for Academic Development*.
(e-mail: adbaume@aol.com)

Pip Bruce-Ferguson is a senior lecturer at Auckland University of Technology, New Zealand.
(e-mail: ferguson@xtra.co.nz)

Glenda Crosling is senior lecturer in Language and Learning Services and Transition and generic skills adviser in the Faculty of Business and Economics at Monash University, Melbourne, Australia.
(e-mail: glenda.crosling@celts.monash.edu.au)

Helen Edwards is a higher education consultant. She was formerly quality adviser, academic programmes, Monash University, Melbourne, Australia.
(e-mail: edwardsh@ozemail.com.au)

Suki Ekaratne is a professor in the Zoology Department at the University of Colombo, Sri Lanka, and is also director of staff development for the university.
(e-mail: suki@eureka.ik)

Joy Higgs is professor at the Faculty of Health Sciences, University of Sydney, Australia.
(e-mail: j.higgs@fhs.usyd.edu.au)

Alison Holmes was a national coordinator for the HEFCE Teaching Quality Enhancement Fund based at the Open University, Milton Keynes, UK and is now Quality Enhancement Manager at Derby University.
(e-mail: alisonjho@aol.com)

Sylvia Huntley-Moore is director of staff education and development in the School of Nursing and Midwifery Studies at Trinity College Dublin, Ireland. (e-mail: shuntley@tcd.ie)

Barbara Grant is an academic adviser and acting director (joint) at the Centre for Professional Development, University of Auckland, New Zealand. (e-mail: bm.grant@auckland.ac.nz)

Veronique Johnston is an academic development adviser at Napier University, Edinburgh, Scotland. (e-mail: v.johnston@napier.ac.uk)

Roger Landbeck has now retired from staff development and is editing the Higher Education Research and Development Society of Australasia's *HERDSA News* from home in Brisbane, Australia. (e-mail: landbeck@ozemail.com.au)

Robyn Lines is manager of the Program Renewal Group at RMIT University, Melbourne, Australia. (e-mail: robyn.lines@rmit.edu.au)

Jackie Lublin is a consultant in academic development in higher education. She was formerly director of the Centre for Teaching and Learning at University of Sydney, Australia. (e-mail: j.lublin@ctl.usyd.edu.au)

Lindy McAllister is associate professor and course coordinator of Speech Pathology, School of Community Health, Charles Sturt University, Australia. (e-mail: lmcallister@csu.edu.au)

Carmel McNaught is professor of Learning Enhancement in the Centre for Learning Enhancement and Research at the Chinese University of Hong Kong. (e-mail: carmel.mcnaught@cuhk.edu.hk)

Peter Muir is a program developer in the Program Renewal Group at RMIT University, Melbourne, Australia. (e-mail: peter.muir@rmit.edu.au)

David Murphy is associate professor and senior course designer in the Educational Technology and Publishing Unit, and acting director of the Centre for Research in Distance and Adult Learning, at the Open University of Hong Kong. (e-mail: dmurphy@ouhk.edu.hk)

Steve Outram is head of quality enhancement at De Montfort University, Leicester, UK.
(e-mail: stephen.outram@dmu.ac.uk)

Anne Oxley is a teaching and learning project manager in the School of Environment and Development at Sheffield Hallam University, UK.
(e-mail: a.oxley@shu.ac.uk)

John Panter is professor and acting staff development manager at Trinity College Dublin, Ireland.
(e-mail: panterj@tcd.ie)

Serge Piccinin is visiting professor at the University of Ottawa, Ontario, Canada. He was formerly professor of Psychology and director of the Centre for University Teaching.
(e-mail: piccinin@uottawa.ca)

Jamie Thompson is principal lecturer and learning, teaching and assessment coordinator at University of Northumbria, UK.
(e-mail: jamie.thompson@unn.ac.uk)

Graham Webb is professor and director, Centre for Higher Education Quality at Monash University, Melbourne, Australia.
(e-mail: graham.webb@adm.monash.edu.au)

INTRODUCTION: THINKING, WRITING AND TALKING ABOUT STAFF AND EDUCATIONAL DEVELOPMENT

We had two main drivers in producing this book on staff and educational development. First, there is a lot of staff and educational development going on. A lot of money is going into development projects and many lecturers are becoming part- or full-time developers. Second, there are very few books on staff and educational development in higher education.

Staff and educational development is a relatively new field of activity in higher education. The history has yet to be written. Staff and educational development as widespread, sustained, widely accepted and systematic activity in higher education is still emergent. Staff and educational development is not yet strongly, and certainly (and happily) not consensually, theorized. It is not yet even strongly 'practised', in the sense that there are few common activities and processes, beyond the three staples – the workshop, the training programme for new teaching staff, and the provision of written and multimedia material – that would be recognized widely as characterizing staff and educational development.

The small number of books on staff and educational development may reflect the fact that both the professional and the academic boundaries of staff and educational development are unclear. As a professional function, staff and educational development abuts, with various degrees of closeness and comfort, teaching and training, human resource development and management, organizational development, management, and the production and implementation of policy and strategy on teaching and learning. Its academic neighbours include the academic counterparts of these professional areas, together with theories and models of learning, teaching and assessment, concerns over academic roles and responsibilities, and action and other forms of research.

We have tended to write *in* our work as developers, producing papers and resources, workshop timetables, learning and teaching strategies and the like. However, only fairly recently have we started to write much *about* our work as developers. The professional and the theoretical issues around staff and educational development in higher education are being addressed, and the literature is thus growing, as it does in any new professional and academic field. Practices are being described and analysed, increasing the amount of literature that is rooted in practice and reaching out towards analysis and theory. At the same time theory is starting to be developed, and its implications for and contributions to practice drawn out. The arch connecting practice and theory is thus being built from both ends, as are most of the best and strongest arches.

However, although we have come rather slowly to *writing* about our work, we note that developers have always *talked* a lot about what we do. In the early days, when we might be the only developers in our institutions, and that alongside other roles, we talked to developer colleagues from other institutions at conferences and meetings about development. Now we are more numerous, we also talk to colleagues within our institution. These conversations address both practice and theory. But we also tell stories, seek responses, explore and make alternative explanations.

Why this book on staff and educational development?

The observation that developers have always talked about their work makes the case study format particularly appropriate for a book on staff and educational development. This book starts with practice. It offers 19 case studies, stories produced by thoughtful staff and educational developers who have interesting and challenging stories to tell.

The reactions we received to our invitations to write a case study were fascinating. We managed to convert some, but alas not all, instances of 'Fascinating idea, love to but, sorry, no time' into acceptances. We met surprise from most authors that we considered their stories worth telling. 'Are you sure? All I did was...' an author would say, following the 'All I did was...' with a remarkable tale of endeavour and achievement, as you will see. We met 'But there's no theory there, it's just what we did', followed by a first draft containing thoughtful analysis and explanation with vivid and valuable insights.

We also occasionally met a difficulty experienced by other editors of books in this series: the difficulty of persuading some developers to write in the narrative style that we sought rather than in a more conventionally academic style. We were delighted when, occasionally after a struggle with the style and format, and perhaps with some vigorous indicative editing from us, case study reporters became fluent and engaging writers of tales about their work as staff and educational developers.

We think we understand some of the reasons for these difficulties and for the subsequent successes. Staff and educational developers speak, or spoke, the language of their first discipline. But developers have necessarily become multi-lingual. We have now learnt to speak the languages of the theory and practice of teaching, learning, assessment, course design, policy, strategy and allied trades in higher education. We speak, perhaps rather less fluently, the languages of the other disciplines with which we work. We certainly must listen very fluently across the full range of disciplines taught in higher education. Increasingly we feel the need to be properly academic about our development work, and for this reason some case study writers may have been reluctant to write in the case study format. But like any other enthusiasts, we still enjoy and draw benefit from telling each other tales of campaigns and struggles and triumphs and disasters, of the insights that flow from these, of the questions and confusions and bright untested ideas and hunches and dreams and plans that remain. In this volume, developers share such tales more widely.

What we mean by staff and educational development

This book is concerned with staff and educational development in the higher education sector – broadly the sector whose institutions offer courses leading to degree-level or equivalent qualifications. We take the primary purpose of staff and educational development to be the improvement of student learning through extending the capabilities of the staff and the institutions that provide higher education. These higher education providers comprise not just higher education institutions but also individuals, groups and local, insti-tutional and increasingly also national educational systems and processes – including courses, teaching, assessment and policies for learning and teaching and quality assurance.

We have said that the main practices of staff and educational development are the workshop, the programme in teaching in higher education, and written and multimedia materials about learning and teaching. These prac-tices also include, as this collection of case studies shows:

- consultancy;
- development projects large and small;
- contributions to institutional and national policy;
- work within particular disciplines and also generically;
- starting from zero through to working in a large and established team;
- teaching;
- both doing and supporting others to do research;
- working in the rough and tumble of institutional life and working in retreat;

- working with staff across an institution from new and part-time staff to senior staff;
- being at many levels in an institution;
- developing and supporting the development of programme, curriculum and teaching and learning methods;
- one-off interventions and sustained programmes over many years.

Who are the developers? As the list of activities above indicates, developers are versatile people. Most have previously been lecturers, some before that practitioners of their discipline outside higher education. Some have previously been researchers. A growing number are managers and staff of educational development projects.

As we see it, the primary defining characteristics of staff and educational development in higher education are:

- the intention to improve higher education, either directly or through the policies and practice of others;
- the emergence of staff and education development as an increasingly academic, scholarly, reflective, theory-informed and professional undertaking;
- the embrace of an eclectic range of models and methods;
- the entry of people from a growing variety of backgrounds into staff and educational development;
- an increasing acceptance of development work by institutions.

Staff and educational development in the literature

The literature on staff and educational development is fairly concentrated, not to say sparse. Nonetheless there is some high quality material well rooted in development practice and increasingly theory.

Angela Brew's 1995 volume *Directions in Staff Development* is an early and still highly valued collection of 14 chapters grouped into three sections, on educational development, staff development and the learning organization. The book combines practical guidance with thoughtful analysis. Webb's *Understanding Staff Development* (1996) encourages us very strongly to problematize the whole idea of development, to see staff development as much more than a technical business of enhancing staff capabilities and supporting institutional change. In a challenging text, the author identifies methodological and ethical issues within the idea of 'developing staff'.

Eggins and Macdonald (2003) undertake a bold quest in seeking *The Scholarship of Academic Development*. Fifteen chapters are organized in two major sections, 'Conceptualizing academic development' and 'Research and academic development', together with an introduction and conclusion. Taken together the chapters mark an academic coming of age for staff and educational development. Individually they offer many productive and challenging models, theories and approaches to a more scholarly academic development.

Helpful texts are emerging, often aimed at new developers. Baume, Martin and Yorke (2002) *Managing Educational Development Projects* is a practical book in which the authors use their experience in many large funded development projects to illustrate how the effectiveness of all stages of a development project can be greatly enhanced.

Kahn and Baume's *A Guide to Staff and Educational Development* (2003) is intended mainly for people relatively new to the profession, although it should also be useful to more experienced developers. It aims to provide advice and guidance, illustrated with examples, on the main staff and educational development methods and issues. It includes needs analysis through planning and running events, consultancy, evaluation, dissemination, ICT, projects, working with the disciplines, national and institutional agendas and reflection. It concludes with that essential but often neglected topic, guidance on self-preservation for the developer.

Enhancing Staff and Educational Development is a companion volume to the *Guide* described above (Baume and Kahn, 2003). It explores topics including developing institutional policy and strategy, leading educational development units and projects, developing and running programmes for new staff, writing for development, and researching and determining the impact of staff and educational development. It also offers a critical overview of development, and explores how developers themselves develop.

The well established journal *Higher Education Research and Development* (HERD) has a strong international reputation. It is published by the Higher Education Research and Development Society of Australasia (HERDSA) and includes articles, review essays, research reports, book reviews, and short critical notes and reflective pieces. It seeks to encourage scholarship that is critically self-aware and to bring fresh thinking and genuinely new strategies to its readers. A review of its 22 (at the time of writing) volumes gives a very good academic and applied overview of the field.

The *International Journal for Academic Development* (IJAD) concentrates wholly on staff and educational development. IJAD has been published since 1996 for the International Consortium for Educational Development (ICED), a network of national educational development networks including the Society for Teaching and Learning in Higher Education (STLHE) in Canada, HERDSA, and in the UK the Staff and Educational Development Association (SEDA). The journal enables staff and educational developers around the world to debate and extend the theory and practice of academic development, in support of the quality of higher education. Papers, case studies and notes are of international interest.

In sum, the literature on staff and education development is expanding, is grounded in practice, is encouraging of theoretical development and is accessible to new developers. At the same time, it reflects the problematic nature of the field.

The cases

We have taken a wide-ranging approach to the inclusion of cases in this book. The book explores 19 cases that cover issues including:

- the nature and meaning of staff and educational development work;
- the roles staff and educational developers adopt;
- how staff and educational developers know how well they are doing;
- the range of scales over which staff and educational developers work, from single interventions to national initiatives;
- working at faculty and discipline level;
- recognizing and rewarding excellence in teaching;
- encouraging inter-professional collaboration;
- changing curriculum approaches;
- what it is like to work across a whole institution;
- developing and implementing national professional accreditation for higher education teachers;
- connecting research with academic development;
- managers as developers.

The cases are written by 21 authors from Australia, UK, New Zealand, Ireland, Canada, Hong Kong and Sri Lanka. The case study authors occupy a wide range of positions, from lone developer in an institution through to national project manager and many in between. The reporters also include senior staff such as professors and heads of departments who undertake development activities as part of their academic role.

The activities reported in the cases range from one-off interventions through to long-haul projects, again with many steps in between. Each case study author tells the story of a critical incident that happened to him or her, and which led to him or her learning and growing on the journey as a staff and educational developer. Each case tells a real story based on an actual case and its resolution. As the cases illustrate, there is no typical path to becoming a staff and educational developer or to doing staff and educational development. The range of people, activities, topics and challenges faced is ever-expanding. Accountability and outcomes are increasingly being emphasized.

As with all books in this series, each case is preceded by an indication of the main issues raised, followed by a summary of the background and setting in which the case study unfolds, and then a series of parts, each of which closes with some questions for you to consider. Each case study concludes with the case reporter's discussion, and perhaps one or two references.

How to use this book

This advice will be broadly familiar to you if you have read and used other books in this series. We have however adapted the advice to meet the particular nature of and audience for this book.

We recommend that, as you read a case, you 'play the game'. By this we mean read first only to the end of Part 1. Then stop reading. Reflect on what you have read. Note your impressions of what is going on, what courses of action could be taken next, what you think will happen next and what course of action you would pursue. Make some notes in response to the questions at the end of Part 1, and in response to other questions that occur to you, and maybe to other questions such as:

- What is going on here?
- What factors may have contributed to the situation described?
- How does the case reporter appear to see the situation?
- What other interpretations might there be?
- How might the situation be handled?
- What sorts of consequences might be expected from these possible actions?
- Given the nature of the participants, how will the situation probably be dealt with?
- Do you face any similar situations?

We then suggest you do the same for Part 2 and for any subsequent parts. In many instances, the questions are specific to the case. After the final part and the case reporter's discussion, you might ask:

- How well was the situation handled?
- What general issues are brought out by the case?
- What do the case and its issues mean for me in my particular situation?

We believe that, as an individual reader, you will gain valuable insights if you use the case studies and discussions in this way. However, we suggest that you will also find it valuable to meet with colleagues to share impressions of the cases and insights obtained from them. The cases can serve as resources for advanced training and development of developers.

Consideration of the cases and issues by groups of colleagues has benefits beyond those that may be obtained from individual reading. In discussions with colleagues, we can confront our own perceptions and readings of cases, and face the possibility that our interpretations may not be shared by others. Justifying our interpretations can bring us face to face with our beliefs about human nature, human learning and the nature of education and development. This can stimulate us to become more reflective about our own practices. We may be challenged to come to terms with alternative conceptions and interpretations of each case. We may be stimulated to re-examine and re-evaluate some of the central features of our own views as we seek to understand each other's interpretations and experiences, and the outlooks that shape them. The discussion sections in this book may provide a starting point; there are further prompts throughout the case studies for quality discussion between colleagues on a wide range of issues.

How do you choose a case study to work on? There can be many ways:

- Because its topic is similar to one you and your colleagues face.
- Because the setting is in some significant way similar to yours.
- Because you feel that the approach taken by the reporter, the issues raised, the methods and ways of thinking used or the conclusions reached will usefully resonate with or challenge you and your colleagues.

Reflection in and on development is crucial regardless of whether you read the cases as an individual or discuss them with colleagues. It is from this effort that you and colleagues are likely to obtain the most benefit from the cases. Interestingly, the case writers themselves, in developing the cases for this book, reported the value they found in reflecting on the development experiences they reported. The authors of the case studies in this book had the courage to discuss openly some of their critical experiences as developers. In doing so they have identified issues which you can continue to reflect on, explore, apply and refine and test against the understandings, beliefs and practices of you and your colleagues.

We hope that your own reflection on development and on the issues raised by the cases presented in this book will be useful. We hope that your reading and reflection will stimulate you to try new approaches to enhance development, which we take to mean enhancing student learning through enhancing the capabilities and approaches of individual and groups of staff and through enhancing educational systems and processes. We wish you every success with your varied and interesting work with your varied and interesting clients, customers and colleagues.

References

Books

Baume, C, Martin, P and Yorke, M (eds) (2002) *Managing Educational Development Projects*, Kogan Page, London

Baume, D and Kahn, P (eds) (2003) *Enhancing Staff and Educational Development*, Kogan Page, London

Brew, A (1995) *Directions in Staff Development*, SRHE and Open University Press, Buckingham

Eggins, H and Macdonald, R (2003) *The Scholarship of Academic Development*, SRHE and Open University Press, Buckingham

Kahn, P and Baume, D (eds) (2003) *A Guide to Staff and Educational Development*, Kogan Page, London

Webb, G (1996) *Understanding Staff Development*, SRHE and Open University Press, Buckingham

Journals

Higher Education Research and Development (*HERD*) published three times a year for the Higher Education Research and Development Society of Australasia (Carfax Publishing)

The *International Journal for Academic Development* (*IJAD*) published twice a year for the International Consortium for Educational Development (Routledge)

SECTION 1

WORKING DIRECTLY WITH TEACHERS

CHAPTER 1

YES, BUT CAN YOU PROVE IT?

Case reporter: Serge Piccinin

Issue raised

The issue raised in this case is how to establish the likelihood of individual teaching consultation leading to lasting improvement and whether such consultation is worth the time and effort.

Background

This case takes places in a large urban Canadian university. The author is an experienced academic and head of the academic development unit. A significant part of the author's work over many years has been individual consultations with academic staff about their teaching.

PART 1

What a dreary, rainy day! And here I sit trying to complete my first annual report of the activities of the teaching centre over the past term. I've provided individual consultation to over 40 academic staff members. And this was just an annual report – between 1990 and 2001, my records showed over 450 out of a total (for 1988) of 840 professors had used the service. It had sure taken a lot of time, energy and effort, but the unsolicited notes from two of the academics expressing appreciation appeared to make it worthwhile. They seemed delighted with the help received, and felt their teaching had indeed improved. They bragged about end of term teaching evaluations by their students. I began to wonder about the others I had seen. Had they also improved?

Perhaps my musings stemmed from a conversation just the previous weekend with a friend, a judge. When I described the kind of work I was doing he expressed scepticism that real, enduring improvement in teaching would really be possible. He stated categorically that good teachers were born and not made. It was a matter of basic personality and it was probably a waste of time to try to change teachers in any significant way.

And what about the senior administrator who also expressed veiled scepticism? The feeling seemed to be that consultation won't lead to enduring change. A few weeks previously a faculty dean had also questioned whether individual consultation could lead to any long-lasting improvement in teaching. He had seen previous self-reports of improvement after consultation, but he doubted the validity of self-reports, particularly when these were gathered soon after consultation. When I mentioned that there were studies indicating the effectiveness of feedback and consultation on teaching, he again expressed doubt and wondered if such studies had been done with real academics presenting real problems.

Prompted by all this scepticism, the question is, how likely is it that my simplest consultation, a single meeting, could really affect deep-rooted views about, and long-practised approaches to, teaching?

I was jogged from these increasingly morose reflections by my secretary who called to say that a professor – I'll call him Professor Smith – had just called. He had attended one of my workshops recently, and now wondered if he could come to discuss his teaching with me. His dean had 'suggested' he come. Oh, oh! I remembered him from the workshop. A senior professor in his department, he has been teaching for a number of years, yet his comments at the workshop suggested he still didn't feel good about teaching. He had railed against the system of student evaluation of teaching we have at our institution.

How likely was it that Professor Smith would change his view, his approach, his teaching, his results, following a consultation? That raised for me broader questions. Can you teach an old professor new tricks? How likely is someone to change how they do things after years of a particular approach? Should the age of faculty member be considered in offering individual consultation?

Have you confronted such questions?
How would you demonstrate the effectiveness of individual consultation to superiors, to colleagues?

PART 2

I held my consultation with Professor Smith, but afterwards I could not get these concerns out of my mind. I was aware of much of the literature on the effects of feedback on teaching, especially when provided together with consultation. At the same time I could see that much of that research was done with small samples, the studies were largely short term, and they were not done with 'real' clients coming to a teaching centre and seeking consultation for 'real' problems. Most studies seemed to have been done with 'volunteers'.

I decided I just had to do something to explore the effects of individual teaching consultation on naturally presenting clients to an academic development centre. But what could I do and how? As I began to focus on this problem it seemed unwieldy, and I recalled comments made by colleagues in other centres: we don't have the time; it is too costly; we don't have the resources to do such a study; don't we already know it works?; and so on. Nevertheless, I felt I had to persist.

I was already keeping count of the numbers of staff requesting and receiving some form of consultation. I wondered whether those seeking consultation were representative of the population of professors in terms of gender, rank, age and discipline. Or were they a special group? This seemed like an important question if one wished to draw any inferences about the effects of consultation.

It seemed particularly important to find an objective method of measuring any change following consultation. Simply having the self-report of recipients did not seem satisfactory. It seemed essential as well that participants in consultation be 'real' clients seeking assistance for 'real' issues they were confronting in their teaching, and not simply volunteers for a research project.

Based on experience to date, it was clear that not all clients came with similar problems and that not all clients were requesting the same services or form of consultation from the teaching centre. The design of any study would have to allow for this. This also raised the question of the relative efficacy of different forms and lengths of consultation. Establishing a control group just would not be possible.

How could I show that consultation and not other factors such as experience over time was responsible for any change in teaching performance? Then, of course, would any improvement endure beyond the immediate post-consultation period? How lasting would any change be?

Beyond these research-based issues, there were practical questions such as the resources necessary (research assistance, funds and so on) to carry out such a study. Clearly such a study would also take time, especially to assess the longer-term effects of consultation. Could I design a study that would work? And would it be worth the effort?

How would you go about undertaking such a study?
What are the major difficulties that need to be overcome?
What would you plan to do after the study had been completed?

PART 3

After much thought, I determined to try to carry out a study. Here is how I dealt with the issues raised.

Participants would be actual clients who came to the teaching centre on their own initiative, requesting consultation related to a specific course they were teaching. Because of the need for a reasonably large sample, data would continue to be gathered until a sample of sufficient size became available. For each client I would record: name and contact information, age, gender, rank, years of teaching experience, discipline, whether tenured or not, source of referral, and presenting problem. I decided not to collect other information or data that might appear unrelated to the request of the client.

An ideal objective measure of change, the end of term student evaluations of teaching, was already available. This measure was chosen because all courses and all instructors are assessed by students on the same instrument after each course and the ratings are publicly available. If there is a perceptible change in teaching performance, then this ought to be reflected in the evaluations of students.

Based on early experience in consultation, I distinguished three types of interventions:

- feedback–consultation (FC) – one interview only discussing topic(s) related to the individual's teaching of a specific course;
- feedback–consultation–class observation (FCO) – feedback and consultation as described above, but in addition observation of the instructor's class followed by one or more sessions providing detailed feedback and suggestions for his/her teaching of a specific course;
- feedback–consultation–class observation and student consultation (FCOS) – in addition to the interventions provided in the FCO category, FCOS incorporated direct student feedback obtained by the consultant at the instructor's request during a private session with the instructor's students.

The particular intervention employed depended on the requested service and on subsequent discussion with the consultant. No particular intervention would be imposed on any client and the intervention used would always be in keeping with the client's wishes. This raises further questions – would all interventions prove equally effective, or would one or another prove more effective? I felt the excitement of a research study taking shape.

What about a control group? I found that it was simply not possible to find a truly equivalent control group when real clients are used. For this reason, I decided to use the participants as their own control group. I did this by noting the instructors' evaluation ratings at the time of consultation and comparing these with their ratings on the same course one to three years prior to consultation. If these were not significantly different, I could reasonably safely conclude any differences in ratings after consultation to be the effect of consultation, rather than simply the result of the passage of time.

To check on the lasting effects of consultation, I examined the ratings obtained one to three years after consultation on the same course. I employed a research assistant to code all the data and to conduct the analyses. It felt important to have an independent person code the data and conduct the analyses so that individuals could not be identified and to avoid any possible contamination of the results.

With all of this set in place, I eagerly awaited the results of the study. What would it show? Had I been wasting my time these past many years with the consultations, allowing my impressions, my developer's optimism, perhaps my selective recall, certainly my enjoyment of the process, erroneously to persuade me of the merits of these consultations? Would I write the work up as a story of success, or as a noble failure? I was at once optimistic and uncomfortable.

What do you think the study will show? Why?

PART 4

Well, what did the studies reveal? What was the result of all this effort?

First of all I was really glad to note that those seeking consultation were quite representative of the population of the teaching staff in terms of gender, discipline and full- or part-time status. They were not an anomalous group, except in one respect: older faculty were under-represented and younger faculty were over-represented in the consultation groups.

The big question – did the consultations and associated activities make a difference? Yes they did! They resulted in significant improvements in teaching, as measured by the change in student ratings before and after consultation.

Did all of the three methods work? Again, yes they did.

Could we see any significant differences between the methods? Yes, we could. The more intensive forms of consultation (FCO and FCOS) led to improvement immediately after consultation.

We checked the results again, addressing my most serious doubt. Could even a very brief consultation (FC), a single interview, lead to significant change? Very clearly from the analysis, yes it could! This result was a particular delight to me; it matched my own impressions, but it was surely counter-intuitive. On close analysis, this result became even more surprising, because this group was already teaching quite well as indicated by their teacher ratings even prior to consultation. One consultation helped the already good become even better.

There were interesting details in the analysis, which raised further questions. Change in this group, the group already teaching well and seen only once, did not appear immediately after consultation as in the other forms, but did appear one to three years later. Why was this?

The observed changes persisted from one to three years post consultation. Do these changes persist over an even longer period of time? But details and further questions apart, we had very strong evidence for the powerful positive effects of individual consultation on teaching, and for the enduring character of the change in the medium term.

Can you teach an *older* professor new tricks? How do older professors learn new tricks as compared to their younger colleagues? I was pleased, and a little bit surprised, to see that both younger and older academics benefited significantly from consultation. But are there differences in the pattern of improvement? Yes. The younger group showed immediate improvement (except for the FC group which showed improvement at the follow-up). The older professors also showed improvement, though the improvement was seen only in the follow-up measurement one to three years after consultation. It may take older professors a little longer to make the changes, but they can, with the help of some patience and understanding, learn new tricks.

Which methods worked better for the older professors? There were insufficient of them to be able to tell.

(Comprehensive reports and published studies conducted are referenced at the end of this case study.)

CASE REPORTER'S DISCUSSION

There were several challenges in conducting the study. First, considerable patience and persistence were required. The study took place over 11 years, requiring commitment over a period of time from both the consultant and research assistants. Finding the funds to cover the cost of the research assistants was another challenge.

Part of the reason the study required so many years relates to the method used to provide a suitable control condition in the study. Many of the new faculty who sought consultation were also new to teaching, and hence had no previous teaching evaluations. Thus, even though many of these new faculty reported that they profited enormously from the consultation they received, they could not be included in the study because they had no previous teaching evaluations that could be used to fulfil the control (passage of time) condition. On the other hand, the very positive results of consultation obtained in the study are strengthened by the knowledge that the clients who met all the criteria for inclusion tended to be more experienced teachers and in all probability, because of this, presented more complex problems.

There is definitely satisfaction in having achieved an important objective: confirming the significant positive effects of consultation. The results of the study help to give credence to the many favourable comments received formally and informally from participants on the benefits of consultation.

If I were starting the study again, what would I do differently? I think there would be real merit in collecting self-report data from the participants and relating these to the more objective results of the consultation. I can think of at least two types of data. Data on the motivational and personality character-istics of the participants would be important, as would be data on what behav-iours the participants feel they actually modified in their teaching as a result of consultation. It might then be possible to relate their perceived changes to the changed teacher ratings provided by their students, as well as to the specific suggestions for change as determined through the consultation process.

The results are an important addition to the body of knowledge in the field. They have also led to a number of practical suggestions for instructional development staff, as well as suggestions for further research. However, I leave it to you to find them in the results above, or in the papers listed below. I shall not elaborate on them here because this is not a case about improving staff and educational development. It is about research and evaluation, about measuring and understanding the effects of what we do as developers, about asking and answering productive questions – and about having the patience and obtaining the resource to find the answers.

When Professor Smith or one of his colleagues next visits me I shall feel much more secure in my ability to help him or her. And I shall rebut the judge's scepticism with evidence.

I have already shown the data to the dean and the senior administrator. Are they persuaded? That's a topic for another case study – on evidence-based management decision making in universities, perhaps!

References

Piccinin, S (1999) The impact of individual consultation on teaching improvement, in *Collected Papers, 24th International Conference on Improving University Learning and Teaching*, Griffith University, Brisbane, Australia, July 1999

Piccinin, S (1999) How individual consultation affects teaching, ch 8 in *Using Consultants to Improve Teaching, New Directions for Teaching and Learning*, No 79, ed C Knapper and S Piccinin, Jossey-Bass, San Francisco, CA

Piccinin, S, Cristi, C and McCoy, M (1999) The impact of individual consultation on student ratings of teaching, *International Journal of Academic Development*, **4** (2), pp 76–88

Piccinin, S and Moore, J P (in press) The impact of consultation and age on student ratings of teaching, *International Journal for Academic Development*, 7 (2)

CHAPTER 2

PROFESSIONAL DEVELOPMENT IN RETREAT

Case reporter: Barbara Grant

Issue raised

This case study raises the issue of designing professional development[1] courses that support ongoing change in practice for both academic advisers[2] and the academics we work with.

Background

This case study is set in an established university in Aotearoa, New Zealand. A fairly experienced academic adviser wanted to assist women academics to write, and also to improve her own academic writing skills, but she was sceptical of the capacity of traditional professional development approaches to achieve her aims.

PART 1

The young academic woman's body language in the lunch-time seminar was particularly disengaged, disgruntled really. I noticed. You do when you're an academic adviser – perhaps the ambiguous and uneasy positioning as colleague and expert makes you sensitive. I watched her leave. It had been a workshop on mentoring and networking, where I had invited a panel of senior women to talk about their experiences and answer questions. Later I read the feedback sheets and one response jumped out at me: for usefulness, 2 out of 7, followed by the comment, 'I attended looking for [strategies] and the seminar didn't help me.' I couldn't help but think that this was the evaluation of the woman I had been watching.

There were other 'nicer' things in the feedback pile too, but for me, this blunt comment was a painful moment of truth. It hooked into my general tiredness (I was about to go on leave) and a pervasive sense of dissatisfaction with my work. Was it making a difference to anyone? More specifically, though, it resonated with my growing sense of the limitations of short seminars and workshops as the basic model for professional development for academics in my institution. I knew from speaking to participants over the years that, by and large, these were not effective mechanisms for supporting change.

To go back a little, between the early and mid-1990s, being aware of the unequal position of academic women in my institution, I organized and facilitated a range of professional development opportunities for them. These were mostly workshops because there was pressure for our centre to provide a 'shop window' for professional development events. The workshops addressed topics such as getting published, setting up a writing life, mentoring and networking, and skills for the writing process. I also ran some ongoing writing groups.

As a feminist academic adviser, I figured some women-only opportunities would be appreciated by my colleagues. Indeed, I looked forward to them, anticipating the different atmosphere, the humour, the candour, and the sense of relief, that I associate with women-only events. The other thing was that I needed these workshops myself. I was inexperienced at getting published. I was also facing real difficulties in keeping my writing going amidst all my other roles, and was uncertain that anyone else would be interested in what I had to say even if I did write about it. But I also had some 'expertise' from many years of working as an academic writing adviser with undergraduate and postgraduate students, so I had some useful models and strategies for tackling writing, and a good deal of enthusiasm for the task, which I thought I could share with my colleagues.

After a good start with the first few offerings, though, I found I was struggling to get enough women to attend. I was also having difficulty finding senior women with enough time to be on the panels, and I needed their depth of experience to give the offerings credibility. I began to wonder if any of this work really made a difference to the struggles many academic women faced in getting writing 'done'. And, from time to time, I faced difficult-to-answer challenges for offering women-only professional development events at all.

So when the participant at the workshop said that it had not helped her, this touched a nerve. I found myself facing a dilemma: Should I bother to go on trying to provide these sort of seminars and workshop, and if not, what could I do?

What do you think are the options now?
What would you do and why?

PART 2

As it happened, around this time I was invited to give a workshop on academic writing for women at another institution. The workshop went well, with a good turn-out and a lively response. After the workshop, one participant, Sue, came up to me and said, 'Hey, Barbara, I think it would be really good if you turned this workshop into a whole day or two-day one, in which we actually did some writing as well as talking about it.' Her enthusiasm was infectious and I liked the idea. But to be honest I was still feeling a bit crushed by my recent experience and, besides, I was about to go on half a year's leave. So we talked for a while, and I promised to get back to her after my leave.

The leave was a good break. During a visit to the UK, I met with a colleague. We talked about her work as an academic adviser working with successful mixed-discipline writing groups. I felt affirmed in the work I was doing and I got some new ideas. I felt recharged!

Soon after returning to work, I contacted Sue. Now we were both enthusiastic, and we began to shape a plan. We decided to organize a five-day residential writing workshop modelled on the idea of a retreat – a withdrawal from everyday life for the purpose of focusing on academic writing. As a child I had watched my mother attend Catholic retreats and return to her large family rejuvenated. I had also attended them myself as a young woman and enjoyed the atmosphere of quiet, focused purpose while being taken care of by others. Sue found a well-established and affordable retreat centre situated on a headland overlooking a large lake and facing snow-capped mountains. It was more or less equidistant between our two universities – about three to four hours' driving time.

We drew up an advertisement and circulated it throughout the women's networks in both our institutions. We decided that 12–15 participants would be enough but, in the end, we only got seven – and then just at the last moment. In addition to numbers, I was worried about outcomes and whether what we planned would be of any value to those who came.

Feeling quite a long way out of my comfort zone (what did I really know about academic writing, how could I sustain a five-day retreat, and so on), I planned the programme carefully (read 'anxiously'). I thought hard about how it could be different from the workshop model of professional development. I also talked at length about the programme with Sue and with another good friend, Avril, who was intending to come (and recruiting her colleagues). In the end, with their help, I made several decisions which reflected both the values I was beginning to attach to my work as an academic adviser and the tensions I was experiencing in it.

First, there was a clear, up-front purpose: 'to produce a piece of academic writing (a conference paper, journal article, book or thesis chapter)'. There were several reasons for this. At this early stage, I felt very responsible for the retreat's success. Attending involved a significant commitment of money, time and energy for the participants. I had no models of other successful academic writing retreats to follow, so felt very nervous about what might happen. I needed to be clear about what I was 'providing'. The other reasons for the clear goal were that I wanted participants to be focused on what they were trying to achieve, and I also wanted to signal real work rather than a holiday.

A second decision was that as much as possible, the retreat arrangements would be negotiated and agreed jointly. This decision came from my ambivalence about professional development being a process in which I am meant to do something to others. At the same time, I realized that I had quite a lot of experience with facilitating group events. In consultation with Sue and Avril, I made suggestions for the programme and let the group decide. This took a bit of juggling, and caused me some anxious moments as I tried to ensure that everyone had input into the decisions.

A related decision was that the retreat be collegial in its process. I did not know enough about writing and publishing to have the retreat workshops depend on me. My previous experience of teaching writing skills had taught me that when you get a group talking together they know much more than any one person, including the academic adviser. I had always learnt more about writing from listening to others. As it turned out, most of those who came were my, Sue's or Avril's friends, so the first retreat 'naturally' had a very collegial flavour.

I decided to attend the retreat in dual roles, as both writer and academic adviser. This was partly my desire to disavow the role of expert, particularly expert academic writer. But also I wanted the retreat to be an opportunity to explore my own writing practices and feelings, and where I could learn about getting published.

The first retreat was an undoubted success, notwithstanding the small group. My worst fears – that some might find it a waste of time or that my inexperience as a writer be shown up – were not realized. We filled out the standard evaluation form of the sponsoring institution in the last session: the women gave the retreat full marks for usefulness, and in the open-ended comments, everyone wrote that they really liked it. They liked being part of a community of writers, sharing ideas, support and inspiration from others. A month later I asked the six participants to write me a letter with their reflections on what had worked well about the retreat for them and what could be improved. Here are some of the things they said.

About the process of negotiating the programme:

I think we all felt comfortable and we all 'owned' the enterprise...
I think the structure we settled on was great. It was the result of an 'almost consensus'.

About the dedicated time and space:

> I felt empowered to find my own space for writing and for sharing ideas. The flexibility of the arrangements for the morning meant that I was very much able to find a working pattern that functioned for me.

About changing views of self and practices:

> The time apart was… a time to open up new possibilities for change – in this case changing my actions and habits as a writer. In relation to the latter, until this week I have always said, 'I am not a writer, I'm an action person.' Yet at an academic and practical level, this has bothered me because I teach action/reflection, expecting my students to do both. For me change often happens when I have time and space to experience the full force of such contradictions. This week did that for me.

About experiencing writing as a social act:

> The small number of women from a range of academic disciplines added richness to the time away and the relationships we formed provided a safe environment in which to critically appraise each other's work. This critical yet supportive environment is something I have found difficult to establish at the university; mainly I think because of the extensive demands on women academics' time which makes it difficult for writing groups to meet regularly.

And an unexpected outcome:

> Our discussion about needing support in academia has led me to ask the famous American professor [x] to be my mentrix. Imagine my anxiety! Yet she accepted and we have agreed upon the arrangement that I can send her three papers a year on which she will give feedback… Without the Taupo talk on the need for a mentor/mentrix I would never have dared to do this.

Since that first retreat in 1997, I have organized two separate week-long retreats at the same venue in each successive year. Most women have returned at least once, many ensure they attend one each year, and some come to nearly every retreat, making this their main writing time. I now also offer shorter three-day retreats at a local venue twice a year.

Through the retreats I have learnt a lot about writing, about new writing tactics to try, and I also get lots of writing done myself. If I can't attend, someone with retreat experience takes my place. I like this because it signals that in the area of ongoing professional development we don't need 'experts' half as much as we think we do. We need time and space to talk to each other in a critical and thoughtful way, with occasional 'expert' input to ginger up our thinking or to offer new ways of doing things.

Occasionally I am challenged about the women-only status of the retreats. My reply is that we, the women who attend, want to keep them that way because we enjoy them. The social dynamics are different when women are 'alone'. There is no reason why a man-only or mixed gender academic writing retreat would not also be an enjoyable and profitable experience, and I am happy for this model and resources to be used.

Going on retreat is a treat for me. Packing up writing materials and computer, sharpening my pencils, tossing in my warmest, most shapeless clothes and hand-knitted socks, buying wine and food, sharing the three-hour drive to the venue with others, catching up with old friends, leaving behind telephones, children, partners, workplaces, students. I love many things about the retreat process: the opportunities for solitude as well as the unexpected connections made with others, the chance to really grapple with the challenges of my own writing, working alongside others who are grappling with theirs, and observing the different approaches they use. Some are so businesslike and unruffled, others fight and resist, yet others seem to daydream their way through a first draft. As well, I value the occasional invitations to enter someone else's writing world and assist her with her work.

The retreats can also be very challenging: I have seen participants really struggle to write. I have felt this myself. Sometimes when you are away, and there is nothing standing between you and your writing, it is frightening because you feel as if you can't do it. Yet as academic women, we must. I have seen women desperately wanting to walk away, and sometimes, though rarely, they have. I have seen women agonize over whether or not this is what they want to do with their lives, and come to decisions to leave the academy. I have seen the strains and tensions of modern academic life play out in group dynamics, sometimes with painful consequences for those involved. To address these difficult moments, I have had to draw on resources and skills that I don't usually use in my work. I have been afraid, I have been angry to find myself out of my depth. Sometimes I have done well, sometimes I have not. Sometimes afterwards, I am exhausted.

The last workshop of every retreat is dedicated to hearing from each woman about how she plans to keep writing following the retreat. Typical plans include setting regular time aside for daily writing, setting up writing groups, or putting aside a day each week. Many women return to the retreats, and some have set up mini-retreats with other local women. Others have established writing pairs or groups which meet regularly to encourage each other in writing. In some cases, participants have used the experience as a model to organize other retreats for academic women in their own institutions or for cohorts of PhD students.

Many have told me that the retreats have made a huge difference to their writing lives. I have found the retreats have helped cement regular writing into my life. These days I also belong to two writing groups, one with fellow PhD students who share a particular theoretical and methodological interest, another with a group of 'junior' academic women from diverse departments. In both groups, our activities centre around sharing writing goals and issues, and reading each other's work to give feedback.

Since the original retreat, there have been 'sister' retreats in other countries (Australia, Fiji, Ireland, South Africa) based on this model, and I receive more requests to run retreats than I can do. But this is a happy dilemma.

CASE REPORTER'S DISCUSSION

The central issue raised by this case is what meaningful academic advising looks like, if it is not the half-day workshop, the individual consultation, or working with a team or department. By meaningful academic advising I mean interventions that make a difference that matters to those we work with.

In my experience, many forms of academic practice are not amenable to the quick fixes favoured by university administrations. Academic writing is a good example. As Sally Knowles and I have written elsewhere (Grant and Knowles, 2000), there is a raft of complex issues associated with whether or not academic women (or indeed many men) write. It is no simple matter to go from being a struggling, even tortured, and unproductive writer to one who is confident and finds pleasure in the act. It seems to require a change in our sense of self which takes time, energy, shifts in beliefs and emotions, and a good deal of encouragement. Academic advising interventions that address these kinds of issues need to be of the 'long fix' kind, somehow inviting participants to commit to the process of change in a sustained way. For that to happen, we have to provide an intervention that responds to a felt need, something that comes from the individuals concerned.

Longer 'fixes', such as the writing retreat, allow new values and principles to operate within professional development. These values and principles may suggest a new role for the academic adviser. For instance, what does it mean to be an academic adviser, as separate from an academic? In my experience, academic advisers are often marginal figures in our institutions. Even when we are also academics, we are often regarded as not 'real' academics or, as Rowland *et al* argue, 'experts of love who have no lover' (1988: 34). Or we are regarded with suspicion as interfering know-it-alls. Andresen (2000) suggests it is a second-order, love–hate relationship, like that between writers and critics. Being institutionally marginal often makes it difficult for us to find a sustaining mode of practice unless we give ourselves over to a mission which, however defined, allows us to feel superior to the academics we are meant to be advising. It is easy then to always place ourselves as experts who can tell academics how to be better at what they do. This is a real danger for us, and one to which our academic colleagues are very sensitive. This is not helped by a common expectation from our institutions that we will further the managerially defined 'quality' and 'excellence' agendas – agendas of which many academics are rightly suspicious.

By contrast, in long-fix interventions that are grounded on felt needs which we share, academic advisers can enjoy the pleasures of collegiality rather than remediality. We can have the pleasures of serving as models of good practice while also showing our willingness to confront our limitations. I don't think we need to deny our expertise, or mourn that we don't have anything to love that we can teach (we do – in my case, a love of good academic writing, among other things). But, at the same time, we need to show we have more to learn, and invite our colleagues to teach and sustain us in reciprocal ways.

What do I learn from the retreats? By participating fully in the writing exercises and work-in-progress seminars, I get all the wonderful support and painful challenging that my colleagues get. By living and working alongside them, I form new friendships and expanded networks that are valuable enrichments to my professional life. In offering workshops and attending other people's workshops, I continue to learn new things about writing and publishing. Even more, I get the courage to continue trying to write, and trying to write better, and my own sense of being an academic is affirmed and challenged and delighted by the experience of being an academic with others. In all of this, I am supported in my work as an academic adviser. I have found my colleagues curious about my work and generous in their praise and criticisms.

Acknowledgements

I would like to acknowledge the contribution made by Sue Watson and Avril Bell to the Tauhara Women Writing Away retreats.

Notes

1 I use the term 'professional development' deliberately, although ambivalently, here. While 'educational development' usually refers to activities related to changing theories and practices of teaching and learning, this case reports changing those of academic writing – a different aspect of the professional practice of an academic.
2 Again my choice of term is deliberate. While some might call me a 'staff developer', I term myself 'academic adviser'. I am critical of the term 'developer' with its connotations of progressive change in a predetermined

direction. As well, I refuse the power relations implied by a scenario in which someone's job is systematically to develop another person.

References

Andresen, L (2000) Teaching development in higher education as scholarly practice: a reply to Rowland et al, 'Turning Academics into Teachers?' *Teaching in Higher Education*, **5** (1), pp 23–31

Boice, R (1997) Strategies for enhancing scholarly productivity, in *Writing and Publishing for Academic Authors*, ed J M Moxely and T Taylor, Rowman and Littlefield, MD

Grant, B and Knowles, S (2000) Flights of imagination: academic women be(com)ing writers, *International Journal for Academic Development*, **5** (1), pp 6–19

McWilliam, E (2002) Against professional development, *Educational Philosophy and Theory*, **34** (3), pp 289–99

Rowland, S *et al* (1998) Turning academics into teachers? *Teaching in Higher Education*, **3** (2), pp 133–41

CHAPTER 3

Mapping the Way

Case reporter: Lindy McAllister

Issues raised

This case study raises the issues of effectiveness and efficiency involved for a head of a programme providing staff development and support for new academics in the establishment of a new course and the development of a new curriculum.

Background

An experienced lecturer is appointed head of a small new speech pathology programme in an Australian university. Her first task is to develop an innovative curriculum focusing on rural practice.

PART 1

'All we do is talk. I just want to get on with teaching instead of spending all this time in curriculum development!'

The words struck me forcefully. I sensed the frustration behind the plea and it reinforced my own frustration with the lack of progress. It seemed such a short time ago that I was merrily thinking, 'This will be fun! Now that I'm head of a new programme I can implement all my good educational ideas, and have a hand-picked staff to do it with. We'll create the best innovative rural speech pathology programme.'

Having managed clinical education programmes in a couple of universities, I had developed a detailed understanding of speech pathology curricula and how they interfaced with the development of clinical competence in students. I had a reasonably good idea of what this new curriculum could look like and how to develop it. However, my role was not to be a one-woman band, but to head up and 'grow' a new academic team, and support their growth as academics, curriculum developers and teachers. Further, although I had a vision for the curriculum, I did not possess all the knowledge and skills needed to develop some of the curriculum threads. For example, although I recognized the need for rural clinicians to be IT literate and knew of the potential for IT applications in teaching and learning, I was at the time of my appointment myself not particularly IT literate. I was an expert e-mailer and could use Word, but had no idea about online chat, forums, Web site development and so on, all of which, four years later, are now a routine part of teaching and learning in the course. I therefore needed to ensure that we recruited staff with these skills, and drew on their expertise in the development of the curriculum and its delivery strategies. We also needed to attract staff with formal qualifications in rural health and experience of alternate service delivery models.

Pat, a part-time lecturer, and I began teaching Year One subjects in 1998, following the direction that had been set in the course establishment documentation. Pat was a new academic who required a lot of support to develop subjects, deliver content and assess learning outcomes. In 1999, Meredith joined us. Meredith was an experienced academic with IT skills and vision for IT use in the curriculum, but someone without experience of rural health and service delivery issues. As a small but committed teaching team, we began to discuss our curriculum and where we wanted to go with it. In 2000, our part-timer became full time, and we added another two staff members. One of these had rural health experience and a vision of what the course could do. The other was an experienced casual lecturer, well versed in the medical model of speech pathology practice, comfortable with traditional approaches to teaching and learning, but not IT literate.

So by the start of the academic year in 2000 we had our core staff, and most of us were ready and eager to continue developing the curriculum. Some of us decided (and the others agreed) at this point to turn the 'mud map' of our curriculum into a fully developed curriculum map, to ensure we covered all the core competencies for speech pathologists, and to weave the threads through the curriculum from years 1 to 4. We began to do this in our fortnightly staff meetings, agreeing to use one hour of these for curriculum mapping.

However, the pressures of academic life as well as those of a small staff with heavy teaching loads meant that we often needed to address more urgent items, and the curriculum mapping would be left. We met at the end of the day, and staff were tired (exhausted in fact) from heavy teaching loads. Gradually it became clear that Chris did not share the vision of developing the curriculum as a group exercise. Chris was mostly silent during group discussions, and her attention was often elsewhere. Chris would rather have been left in peace to teach assigned subjects the way she had always done, and to use what little precious time there was to do things other than curriculum development. The result was that I found it generally quite hard to engage Chris in being a 'member of the staff', as opposed to an individual lecturer.

On the other hand, the rest of the staff such as Pat and Meredith were stimulated by all the ideas and had wonderful ideas of their own. It fired their creativity to do more and different things with their students. They went off on tangents that created exciting learning opportunities for their subject area, but such ideas failed to create a coherent, whole curriculum. Sometimes these good ideas were only partially translated into reality, and staff and students would be left with fall-out from sketchy curriculum concepts half-baked into teaching and learning activities. Staff would also exhaust themselves with over-reaching and doing too much. Staff new to academia who were already struggling with their time management found such a demanding activity as curriculum mapping to be too time consuming. So the task of curriculum mapping lapsed until we had 'more time'.

While acknowledging this reality, I felt increasingly frustrated with the slow progress of the curriculum development and mapping endeavour. And I was puzzled by Chris's lack of interest. I appreciated that not all academics are as passionate about this stuff as others, but resented the comment that 'All we do is talk', and the implication that we were wasting our time. I knew Chris valued students' opinions and was 'a great lecturer'. 'Why can't Chris show as much enthusiasm for supporting the teaching of others?' I thought as I drove home after another staff meeting where yet again little progress had been made.

Reflecting on the question jolted me into confronting the lack of shared values and understanding in our group. Much of the knowledge I had about curriculum and professional standards was the result of my previous experiences, and in the main it was 'tacit' knowledge. I began to realize that Chris didn't understand the importance or the process of curriculum development. I would need to take more time and effort to articulate my beliefs, reasons and motivations for doing this curriculum development and mapping. I also realized that I would need to talk with Chris about her resistance to the process and her wish to be a 'freewheeler' in the staff. This was a prospect I didn't relish.

While we waited to find the elusive 'more time', cracks in the foundation and infrastructure of the curriculum were starting to show. Feedback from our end-of-semester student forums pointed to problems with and gaps in the curriculum. Some topics were repeated while others were omitted. We assumed prior knowledge and skills for topics or assessments, only to find that the foundation knowledge and skills required were not covered when, where or by whom we thought. When we looked at the failure of students in the third year to do assignments that required a long piece of writing, involving analysis and critique of literature and ideas, we discovered that nowhere in the course prior to this did we set an assignment that involved a long essay or required an analytical approach to text. We even found a gap in teaching and assessment of one of the required clinical competencies, when we were putting together course accreditation documentation for the professional association.

This was the final straw for me. If the profession could not accredit our course, it would be a major loss of credibility for us. We needed a curriculum map quickly!

How do you get people to commit to a process of curriculum mapping?
How can the problem of 'no time' be overcome?

PART 2

It would have been easier at this point to finish the curriculum map myself or with those colleagues who were clearly committed to it. It would certainly have been faster. And given their respect for my competence and authority as programme head, it then may have been possible to impose this curriculum on the other staff. However, this is not my style of leadership and I would have been uncomfortable with doing it. Also, there was my responsibility to support the staff development of others to enable them to understand and own the curriculum development. Apart from anything, I also really wanted this to be a whole-team effort. A small teaching team involved in the process of building a new course and a new vision cannot afford to have groups – those in the inner circle versus those in the outer circle. Working as a team was philosophically and pragmatically important to me.

The view that we needed to get on with and complete the curriculum map was discussed in a staff meeting. Most of the staff felt they were committed to the process but that we needed blocks of time, rather than to try to do it one hour a fortnight. They also felt that it would be better to do it off-campus, where we would be free from the interruption of students knocking on the door, and the tyranny of e-mail, phones and committee meetings. We began to look for days where everyone would be free in the intra- or inter-semester breaks. Because of school holidays, conferences, the needs of families and so on, finding common 'free time' was not easy. We finally decided that we would use a weekend, that we would go away from campus, and that to avoid neglecting our families, we would make it a family-fun weekend. We planned a timetable that saw us working solidly in the mornings and afternoons, but with free time at lunch for families to join us, and with late afternoon and evening time off for fun as a staff group and with families involved.

Where to go on our curriculum planning retreat was another issue. We would have to fund this ourselves, as money in the university was tight, and this exercise did not fall under research development or normal professional development activity. Chris came to the rescue. She volunteered a relative's farm, about two hours south of the campus.

The other staff and their families stayed in a very cheap hotel nearby, travelling out to the farm in the early morning for three or four hours' work before our families joined us for lunch and exploration of a working cattle property. After another three hours of work in the afternoon, the families again joined us for more farm fun. We all met for dinner at the hotel in the evening, sitting around the fire afterwards, playing pool, listening to music, dancing, chatting or continuing work-related conversations. Partners and children found plenty to do during the day, and we all enjoyed each other's company at night.

This weekend was a turning point for us as a staff. Playing 'host' allowed Chris to 'lead' the activity, and free of the pressures of normal work routine to be more fully engaged in and enjoy the process. As a result of the ideas and encouragement received that weekend, Chris was stimulated to change radically the way she taught her subjects. She changed from traditional lecture-based delivery to a modified problem-based approach. She began to seek opportunities to talk with the rest of the staff about teaching, sharing the challenges they experienced, asking advice, and generally wanting to know what 'we' stood for and where 'we' as a staff were heading.

Having about 12 hours of focused time allowed us to make significant headway with the curriculum map. We could all now comfortably talk with each other about 'our curriculum' and 'our subjects'. We knew where the foundation knowledge and skills sat relative to individual subjects, and what generic competencies we should be aiming for in addition to clinical competencies in any particular subject, so that curriculum threads could continue to be woven and curriculum goals achieved.

It also gave us time to really talk to each other about our lives, and personal and professional histories and interests. We discovered a lot about each other that has strengthened friendships and good working relationships. We 'bonded' as a team. We also had time to talk about our common research interests, and several research projects have arisen as a result of that meeting.

Further, our families gained an insight into the demands of our work and our aspirations as a team, which they felt they could continue to support by keeping the 'home fires burning' as we worked the long hours necessary to establish the new course. Friendships between families were forged, further identifying them as part of something exciting, and providing social opportunities for new families who had all relocated into the area because of their partners' and parents' careers.

CASE REPORTER'S DISCUSSION

This case highlights several issues around staff and curriculum development. First, curriculum development takes knowledge and expertise in the processes involved. Had I as head of programme not had that knowledge and some experience, the process of developing a cohesive, effective curriculum, which fulfilled the course mission, provided a quality learning experience for the students, and met professional association requirements, would have been a lot more painful, disjointed and protracted for all involved. Not every person coming into the role of head of a course has this background, and yet at no time did the university offer the course and its staff any support and input from curriculum specialists. In the end we did ask for and receive some support, but only because we knew what questions to ask and what was possible. The provision of expertise to support the processes that we self-generated needs to be routine in universities offering new courses. It is possible for heads with knowledge and experience to lead curriculum development, but they need support to do so.

Second, curriculum development and mapping takes time. Staff need to be supported with more than 'motherhood statements' from their employers that curriculum mapping is a good idea, and provided with time out and financial support for the process. While we were prepared to do this in our own time and at our own expense, this should not be the routine expectation.

Third, and more positively, going on 'retreat' to work on the curriculum proved to be an excellent strategy, not only to find a block of quality time free from distractions and fatigue, but also to provide an opportunity for staff to bond as a team. The beneficial outcomes of our curriculum development retreat extended far beyond the main purpose, into teaching and research collaborations, and the strengthening of a harmonious, energized workplace.

Fourth, it is always a challenge to get all academic staff heading in the same direction at the same time, and equally committed to the task at hand. Who was it that once said 'trying to manage academics is like trying to herd cats'? The task of herding cats is stressful for all programme heads, especially for those new to the role. I found my values and conceptions about my role were constantly challenged. I would have appreciated opportunities to debrief and explore what was happening with a 'mentor', but none was offered. No doubt one would have been provided had I requested that, but buried as I was in the day to day rush of my head of programme role, perhaps having an assigned mentor with expectations to meet regularly would have been worthwhile.

Finally, less tangible but very real rewards have been the development of a cohesive teaching team that understands the breadth and depth of its endeavour and derives significant personal and professional satisfaction from this. The staff have a clear sense of themselves as pioneers of new directions in speech pathology education. Development as curriculum developers and scholars has been rapid both for the fledgling academics on the team, and for those who came with more experience. Collaborative teaching and research activities have developed, and staff are now well placed to devote more time to the development of their research profiles, and to the development of graduate research student programmes.

Staff have continued to work hard on development of 'our curriculum', and there have been rewards for this effort and commitment. The course has to date fulfilled its mission to prepare graduates for rural and remote practice, with 75 per cent of our graduates choosing to work in rural and remote areas, and with employers providing us with excellent feedback on their skills and attributes. Our students have enjoyed being partners in the development of the course, through participation in feedback forums, subject reviews, and course and subject questionnaires. They have been unstinting in their praise – and their criticisms! – all of which has helped us refine the curriculum. The course went through the professional association's accreditation process with ease, and with compliments on its impact in changing the direction of the profession. Some 20 invited and peer-reviewed articles and national and international conference presentations with staff and students (see for example McAllister, 2000) have presented descriptions and evaluations of innovations in the curriculum, including the development of a multi-disciplinary primary health care subject, the use of IT chat rooms to support fieldwork, and the use of community-based placements in rural health services and in resource-poor settings in Australia and abroad.

Our curriculum map is a 'work in progress'. Student feedback each semester leads to minor revisions and course revision due in the next year or so will no doubt necessitate more major revision to our curriculum map. Another of the many remaining challenges for us is to publish as a team our experiences of the process of curriculum development and mapping, and the teaching, learning and staff development outcomes of that endeavour.

As head of this programme, when I reflect on the last four years, I am often amazed at what we as a team have achieved in developing a new course from the ground up. At a personal level, I am surprised that I have been able to combine staff development, curriculum development, teaching, research and administrative roles without too much angst (just a lot of long days and a few sleepless nights as I mulled over the challenges). Engagement in the processes of curriculum development and mapping described in this case study has strengthened some, and developed others, of my values and conceptions about my role as head. It affirmed for me my belief in the importance of inclusion and team building, and in persistence in working towards the achievement of these.

The process also strengthened my belief in taking responsibility and initiative for what you want. We may have waited a long time for time relief or resources to complete our curriculum map. The fact that we invested our own time and money in the task enhances both the ownership and the pride we feel in our work. In addition, I came to better understand the importance of 'airing' values and beliefs; of 'confrontation' if necessary; of tackling problems head on; and, that the short-term 'pain' can have long-term 'gain'. This process also developed my creativity in finding strategies for engagement and roles (such as 'host') for less involved staff that facilitate their involvement and enjoyment of the process.

Final confirmation of the value of the process came when our programme won the Vice Chancellor's 2002 Group Award for Excellence in Teaching.

Reference

McAllister, L (2000) Educating for the future: the need for new goals of health science education, *ACQ: Issues in Language, Speech and Hearing*, February, pp 5–7

CHAPTER 4

ARE TEACHERS REALLY RESEARCHERS?

Case reporter: Pip Bruce-Ferguson

Issues raised

This case explores issues concerning teachers using their own teaching practices in order to develop a research programme.

Background

A well established New Zealand polytechnic was granted degree awarding status in 1991 and now offers a range of degrees. Because of this, staff were required to engage in research, where this had previously not been an expectation. The situation caused considerable concern about workload, and about issues of balance and identity in the organization. The case reporter is a staff developer working in the polytechnic.

PART 1

'I don't know why you bother. Haven't you got enough to do already?' This was my friend Anne's comment as I explained that I was commencing doctoral study into an effective way of developing a research culture at our institution. My interest had been sparked several weeks before, when Joan left an urgent voicemail message asking to see me. I was then a staff developer in the institution, and had worked with Joan in her early teaching practice development. I could hear tension in Joan's voice, and wondered what on earth had upset her. I'd observed her teaching as part of her teacher training, and found her to be a conscientious, committed staff member, making good progress in what was a new career for her, after years of professional practice. I phoned back, made a time to see her, and settled down to wait for her arrival.

When Joan entered my office, I could see that the tissue box would be needed. She was very stressed, very upset, and legitimately concerned for her future employment. Joan's boss had told her that because her course had gone into the new degree, she would have to do research if she wanted to continue to teach that course, and furthermore she would need to upskill her academic qualifications. Joan already had a three-year professional qualification and lots of work experience. She couldn't face the prospect of further study, plus research, on top of what was already a heavy workload. 'It's just not fair!' she sobbed. 'I know I'm a good teacher; I work all the hours God gives me to do the best for my students, and now this!'

I listened sympathetically, and tried to suggest ways in which Joan could work the issues through with her boss. I suggested ways of researching her teaching practice without having to engage in 'traditional' or 'scientific' research which was the approach her profession usually valued. Taking that route would mean months, if not years, of learning.

Unfortunately, over a period of months Joan decided the task was too great, and left the organization. Her situation, though, alerted me to the stress and concern being experienced by many other staff in the organization, and I started to listen and reflect even more carefully than I usually did. The research requirement seemed to be creating the most concern. Staff reckoned that you could research, or you could teach, but to do both simultaneously was too much to ask. I wondered what I could do.

What possibilities do you think there are for action?
What do you think will happen next?
If you have faced the situation of having desperate and distressed staff in your office, how have you coped?

PART 2

I had to admit that I'd 'failed' Joan. An organization-wide imperative, imposed by government policy, was too much for me to change, and I couldn't do anything fast enough to help her. But I still thought the idea of staff engaging in research into their own teaching was a good one.

I recognized that I'd need some personal motivation to help me with the task, and I'd been looking for a suitable topic for a PhD thesis. With considerable trepidation, as I had only a short course in action research to my credit prior to enrolling in the doctorate, I chose to investigate the benefits of action research as a way of helping the staff to meet their research requirements, and simultaneously to help build a research culture that would 'fit' into the organization's practical orientation.

I had to find a 'win–win' situation for the staff, as much as possible, given their concerns about heavy workloads. New staff were required, as part of their conditions of service, to undertake 12 weeks of teacher training alongside their teaching practice. All but three of those weeks were prescribed courses that were compulsory. Accordingly, I introduced an optional action research course (70 hours equivalent), took it through the academic processes, advertised and taught it, initially in conjunction with a colleague who had previously taught action research. This would enable staff to meet an existing employment demand, to learn research skills, to improve their practice (which all good staff developers seek to do!) and, if they wished, to produce publishable research. It would build on their own practice, which the good teachers already valued highly, without necessarily being seen as a 'distraction' from that practice, which was the perception of more traditional research.

I planned to interview the students who had graduated from the course a year down the track, in order to investigate how effectively it had helped them to learn research skills which they may previously have lacked, how it had benefited their classroom practice, and whether it had helped them to meet research requirements.

One of the benefits of being a staff developer is that you are often able to take a 'macro' view of the organization. I recognized that grass-roots action alone might not be enough, if the research directions that the organization chose to follow ruled out classroom-based research as legitimate. Accordingly, I lobbied and had myself elected as one of two staff representatives to our new Research Committee. From that position, I was well placed to argue for teacher-researching along with the more traditional research approaches that others were advocating. This classroom-based research is now firmly embedded in our definition of research.

What do you think of the approach taken? Was it what you expected?
How effectively can staff development meet individual and institutional goals
at the same time?

CASE REPORTER'S DISCUSSION

This case is probably the 'biggest' situation I had to deal with as a staff developer at the polytechnic. The impact of degree awarding on the organization, seized on with glee by some, had major implications for workload and identity. The workload issue was identified in Joan's story. Most of our staff, up until the degree-granting era, had been employed because of their strong professional and vocational backgrounds. These were valued as giving credibility to their teaching, and enabling them to help their students to make close links between the theories they were being taught, and practical work experience.

However, the degrees changed all that. There's an unwritten rule that says if you teach in a degree, you need to have a qualification one level higher than that on which you teach. Therefore there was a huge need for staff to upgrade their qualifications, which meant study on top of existing workloads. (The theory was that workloads would diminish to allow for the study, but that didn't seem to happen much in practice!) Then there was the common perception that research was 'done by men in white coats in laboratories', or by exalted beings with fancy degrees in ivory towers. Many of the staff did not identify research as being what they could or should be doing.

When I interviewed five of our 'foundation' staff who had been with the organization since its inception, three of them clearly stated that research belonged 'over on the hill over the river' (ie, at the university); that 'Research was seen as belonging to the universities', and 'Can we do it better than the university? I don't think so.' But the fourth stressed the benefits of research illuminating practice, describing how he constantly strove to improve his practice via research, but wouldn't publicize it. The fifth foundation staff member was the principal, who had come up through the ranks and had quite a different understanding of the place of research from the other four. He backed up the researching teacher's feelings about not publicizing research that was done in classrooms, though, saying, 'We do it, we don't talk about it.'

I had correctly discerned that classroom-based research was happening, and that the reflective practice I observed good teachers using was a sound basis from which to introduce them to action research. But alongside this sound discernment, I had overlooked the culture of some departments, such as the two from which our foundation staff were drawn. They see talking about what you have developed as a form of bragging, and therefore my feeling that action research could lead to publications was faulty. They were quite happy to discuss action research but didn't want to get publications out of their work.

Two other action researchers from very different areas of the institution discussed this reticence. A catering tutor described the criticism he perceived from colleagues when he used his new research skills to critique some research done by an outside person, and a computer tutor described her feelings of anxiety when she offered to run a seminar for colleagues at an in-service day. 'They are just going to sit there and think what's she doing, standing up there? What's she got to say?' But doing the course gave her the confidence to go ahead regardless.

So I'd overlooked the impact that my 'good idea' would have on the identities of the staff. New Zealand has the 'tall poppy' syndrome. We tend to be very critical of people who excel in particular areas, often seeing them as braggarts who have forgotten their roots, or who have excelled at the expense of those they've left behind. The role of a researcher requires us to put our work in the public domain for examination and critique, and this is probably the hardest issue that our staff had to face. They haven't had enough research experience to recognize the excellence that many of them demonstrate in their practice, and about which they can validly write, so they feel inadequate when asked to stand up and speak about their work. Yet, when they finally do go to conferences, many come back amazed at how unexceptional much of the work presented is, and how far ahead New Zealanders are in some areas. So perhaps I should have taken that reticence into consideration more, perhaps by easing people into research through collaborative projects initially.

The alert reader at this point is likely to say, 'Hang on, isn't action research collaborative by nature?' Well, yes! But I shot myself in the foot in my course design, and unwittingly limited possibilities for collaboration at the outset. 'Oh my friends, be warned by me!' as Hilaire Belloc famously wrote in one of his poems. The course generally attracted only one staff member (student) per department, and I'd set up the teaching component so that the staff members constructed their research question on the third day of the course, before returning to their departments. So when they got back, they usually found that the question that fascinated them didn't push anybody else's buttons, or that their colleagues were too busy or anxious about participation to get involved. Accordingly, most of my action researchers had to work alone. This made the catalytic nature of the research, which I'd fondly anticipated building towards a thriving research culture, non-existent. It further made it hard for new researchers to stand up and declare what they'd done, to publish it either in their departments or at conferences.

In some respects I 'got it right': the reflective practice common in the institution well underpinned my choice of action research as a familiar way of introducing staff to research practice, and was compatible with my role as a staff developer. Another way in which I got it right was my attempt to ensure that Maori staff could participate equally in the approach. New Zealand has a mixed cultural environment, with the Maori people as the indigenous inhabitants. Our Treaty of Waitangi, signed in 1840, requires the Crown to ensure equal partnership, participation and protection for Maori ways and interests, a requirement that has been ignored more than carried out over much of our history. The polytechnic where I worked is located in a strong Maori tribal area, and one reason I was keen to introduce action research is that I had observed similarities between traditional Maori ways of investigation, and the action research approach. I was pleased, then, when Maori students joined others in the course over a number of years. I was even more pleased when one said, 'It is a process that we are doing anyway.' She found that action research helped her and her colleagues to investigate the delivery of an off-site programme, and to improve the ways in which it operated.

There is an issue here for staff developers to consider, in an increasingly globalized and mobile world. How do we ensure that our practice is as inclusive as possible? How can we work to recognize differing perspectives and practices in our programmes? In fact, I 'got it wrong' with my Maori action researchers! Although Maori is an official language in New Zealand, I did not make it clear that the action research project could be submitted, written in Maori language. After a Maori-speaking student pointed this out to me, I learnt from this mistake.

My intuition that action research – indeed, any classroom-based research – would be a way for staff to meet research requirements while simultaneously building on their known and valued classroom practice has generally been successful. Our Research Register over the past five or six years demonstrates a variety of classroom-based research projects that have been carried out and published in journals, books or at conferences. This is an example of staff development assisting both individuals and the institution to meet their goals.

CHAPTER 5

And the right answer is...

Case reporter: Jackie Lublin

Issues raised

The issues raised in this case are the reluctance of teaching staff to acknowledge that assessment involves know-how and skill, and the difficulty of encouraging staff to change their behaviour around assessment.

Background

The case reporter was invited by a new professor to conduct a one and a half-day workshop on assessment for the staff in the veterinary science faculty in a university in Europe. The professor organized his somewhat reluctant new faculty into the workshop on assessment as part of a larger programme of curriculum reform. The case reporter had previously worked with the professor in Australia.

PART 1

'Talking is not permitted.'
'Don't let your neighbour see your work.'
'Pens down, time is up.'

These were instructions being given to a group of colleagues, not students. What on earth was I doing? What were they doing? A group of veterinary science staff were doing a real test under exam conditions. But why get them to do this, and how did I get them to agree to do it?

About two-thirds of the faculty's teaching staff had agreed to attend this workshop on assessment and I had accepted the invitation willingly, while at the same time wondering if discipline and cultural differences might outweigh the commonality of university assessment rituals. I did not need to worry: in general, the faculty's attitudes and procedures in teaching and assessment were quite familiar, with formal exams being very important as the major form of summative assessment. Some staff members had expressed concern to me that perhaps the faculty could be doing better in assessing its students, but there had clearly been little real commitment in the past to exploring alternatives to the way things had always been done.

My briefing told me that, while a few of these staff were genuinely interested in exploring alternative and better ways of assessing their students, many were uncommitted, defensive and apparently reluctant to change. Most apparently believed that assessment was something you thought about fleetingly at the end of the course, for which no expertise was required and for which minimal preparation was required. The challenge was to confront these staff and if necessary to shock them into taking assessment seriously and educate them about ways of doing it better. But what could I do that would sufficiently disturb them and challenge their assumptions? I decided that the most confronting thing I could get them to do would be to sit for an exam.

Like many other conservative faculties whose staff were looking for ways of assessing more students, this vet faculty was making extensive but uncritical use of objective tests using MCQs (multiple choice questions) for summative purposes. I decided that this would be my point of entry. If I could demonstrate to faculty staff that an apparently uncomplicated MCQ exam could be deeply flawed, and why this was the case, then I thought that their eyes might be opened to some of the consequences for students of their not paying attention to the technical aspects of assessment.

It is one thing to take part in a cerebral discussion of the issues involved in examining using MCQs, but it is an entirely different thing to demonstrate these through a concrete experience. Where would I get such an exam? I was not a vet, I had no time to commission an exam paper, and anyway I wanted it to be as authentic an experience as possible for this group of vet faculty teachers. I decided I would go to the Web. There I came across an examination paper in a first-year first-semester subject from another university's veterinary science faculty. The subject dealt with whole animals rather than with elements of basic science. At this elementary level of knowledge I thought that the test should be a breeze for academic vets (although of course there were also bioscience specialists on the vet faculty).

However, even I, a non-vet, could see that the MCQ section of the paper seemed to be rather idiosyncratic. If it was flawed, then it was perfect for my purposes. Best of all, it was a genuine exam paper. So I decided to administer this test to the assembled faculty staff I was working with in the workshop, if they would agree to it, and I decided that I too would do the test.

With a bit of sweet-talking on my part, the participants thought the idea of their doing a first-year exam might be a bit of a giggle, and all took part. I administered it under quasi-exam conditions, making a joke of it, but stressing nevertheless that this was indeed a section of a real first-year exam paper.

The test consisted of 12 MCQ items (questions), each with one 'right' answer (known as the key), and three distracters – that is, answers that are incorrect but that are credible as possible alternative answers. If the test was any good then I would not score anything much, and the vet faculty staff would do very well on a first-year test about whole animals. If the test was no good then all hell might break out. I held my breath and went ahead.

What do you think happened as the staff took the test?
How do you think the staff reacted after taking the test?
What do you think happened next?

PART 2

'Oh, dear.'
'What on earth does that mean?'
'I can't do this.'

I was relieved to hear the sorts of sub-vocalizing that goes on when people encounter something they are not expecting. Since I was sure they expected that they would have no trouble with the test, I reiterated several times that this was a genuine first-year exam paper, administered to real students at the conclusion of a semester's work.

'Time's up. Lay down your pens. I'll collect your answer sheets,' I intoned. I collected an answer sheet from each participant and then collated the results so that distributions could be scrutinized across the range of four possible responses (called 'cells') for each question. The point about an MCQ question is, of course, that there should be agreement among experts about the right, correct or best answer, and this was a group of experts I was working with. If this was a good test then the key and the distracters should be agreed for each item.

What were the results? They were terrific for my purposes, which was to confront staff and challenge their comfortable lack of interest in the pitfalls of constructing such tests. There were 12 MCQ items in the test and 19 respondents, excluding myself.

Six of the 12 questions scored between 12 and 19 in the one cell. I decided arbitrarily (and generously) that these results constituted the key or 'correct' answer for each of these six questions. However, the results from this group of vet faculty teachers for the remaining six questions were far more haphazard, with a spread of scores in each of the four cells in each MCQ. In other words, among this group of experts there was no agreement about what constituted the right answer to at least half of these exam questions pitched at first-year students. Furthermore, even I, someone with no background or knowledge in the area, scored 4 out of 6 in the first six questions, where there was agreement on the right answer.

As you might imagine, there was much consternation and bewilderment among participants when I gave them the results. I don't know how much of this was due to the sort of response we might privately have in such a situation, where we wonder if it is due to our own inadequacy, or how much was due to a feeling of having been 'had' by the paper itself. I was even accused of making the test up in order to produce these results. However, I had taken the professor in charge into my confidence before the session, and he vouched for the fact that the paper did really exist and was on the Web. So there was no wriggling away from the difficult question which I then posed: 'How is it possible that an exam paper can produce such a range of results from faculty teachers in a situation where there should be unanimity about the correct answer, and where a layperson can score so well without experiencing the teaching in the subject?'

I immediately took pains to assure staff that it was not they who were foolish, deluded or wrong in having produced these results – after all, they were the discipline experts and this was a first-year paper. I said that I would demonstrate that these disastrous results occurred because of the nature of the MCQs themselves. It must be said that I now had their full attention – my shock tactics appeared to have worked, so the first objective, to cause them to pay attention, had been fulfilled.

We worked through the 12 questions. I think it is always an unpleasant surprise for staff to look closely at the wording of their own exam questions and have to acknowledge that they are ambiguous from the point of view of the student, or that they do not actually express what the teacher had in mind. Luckily it could be done at one remove in this case, as no one in the group was responsible for the wording of this MCQ paper, so these staff could look dispassionately at the items without defensiveness or the need to justify or explain.

It quickly became clear to the group that some of the fault did indeed lie in the idiosyncrasy of the wording and thus of the thinking which lay behind these MCQs. But I wanted to demonstrate that poor test construction was the major cause of these results. Two or three of the questions were worded in a reasonable way (these were the ones where there was a consensus about the correct answer). But when we scrutinized the questions closely it was possible to classify most of the rest as '*Guess what is in my mind*'.

These were the questions that might otherwise be thought to be trivial or even nonsensical. My vets could not make head nor tail of these questions, and could not agree on the right answer, but students who had made a point of attending to the eccentricities of the lecturer who set the questions would probably do well on them.

'I want to maintain my reputation as a humorist, so I will throw in a quite ridiculous distracter now and then.' However, patently ridiculous distracters can immediately be eliminated by anyone, including students and me, thus leaving the examinee with less to choose between and therefore more chance of achieving the right answer or of guessing correctly.

'I know the right answer.' There was general agreement among my group of vet faculty teachers that at least one of the questions had no right answer (or 'best' answer), and that at least one other question clearly had more than one correct answer. How are students supposed to cope with this?

When we looked at the questions this way, it became obvious why the group had struggled with particular questions. It also became clear that students who attended to the personal quirks of the teacher, who learned the material they were taught without query or who were exam-savvy, would probably do quite well on this exam. All the questions called for no more than the recall of basic information, or in terms of Bloom *et al*'s (1956) well-known scheme for classifying levels of thinking, they were all at Level 1. And why did I do so well? Life experience and intelligent guessing. Altogether a sorry reflection on the fallibility of MCQs.

I summed up the educational value of this flawed test by asking how much confidence one could have that a score from this test would be an accurate reflection of a student's ability in the subject. The faculty members agreed that what a good score would indicate in this instance would be primarily the student's ability to play the exam game as laid down by the lecturer. But what to do about it? And how to slip them the knowledge they would need in order to write fair and unambiguous MCQs when they themselves were producing MCQ tests? It is one thing to recognize the frailty of others, another to change oneself. How could I use this experience to produce behavioural change with the individuals in this group?

What are the possible courses of action at this point?
What are the dangers in moving to the next step?
What would you do next?

PART 3

'OK,' I began, 'I now invite each of you to go ahead and produce one MCQ item relating to your area. Think about what you want your students to do. Is it more than merely recalling facts?' I gave the participants as much time as could be spared to write their MCQs, and then invited them to form groups of six and to work through each other's questions without knowing the key in advance, and then to discuss the results.

In the best of all worlds there would have been time for a debrief looking in detail at one or more MCQ item from each group, the changes made to the item as a result of the group's discussion, and the insight gained by the writer about his or her intentions in setting the question. In other words, the need for and the benefits of a trialling process would have been consciously identified. As it was, the session ended with discussion still in progress. Several people commented in the final short plenary that they had had no idea about what hard work it was to write a credible MCQ. That was gratifying.

However, it is what comes out of a workshop that is more important than what goes on during the workshop. Eight months later I asked the professor if there had been any outcomes from or response to that MCQ experience in his faculty. He told me that:

- There was now a greater awareness of idiosyncratic issues, and definitely more stringent attention to language use in exams.
- Draft exam papers were now reviewed by more than one staff member.
- In one department 'a move in the direction of the use of MCQs was curtailed as a result of the (workshop) discussion'.
- The Faculty's Examinations Committee commissioned an internal paper on constructing MCQs. Included in the paper is this paragraph:

> To avoid one person's prejudices and errors, test your MCQs on colleagues. A subsequent discussion on results should improve the MCQs. It is essential not to let your ego get in the way of such an exercise. Care must be taken so that as nearly as possible the student will read the question in the same sense as the examiner. The examiner should know exactly what he/she wants to ask and be determined to produce a form of words that cannot be misunderstood.

CASE REPORTER'S DISCUSSION

The case raises several issues of central concern to staff developers working with academic staff in a voluntary environment. Perhaps the most important is the need to avoid the sorts of learning situations we consciously try to change in the staff–student situation. I mean by that, the overwhelming seductiveness of hearing our own voices, and the seductiveness of being the person out at the front with the power. If a staff development session turns into a didactic monologue about, say, the need for student activity as an aid to student learning, then the role modelling will be at odds with the message. There is no prize for guessing which message the staff audience will retain. Consequently, it seems to me that experiential learning is as necessary and effective for academic staff as it is for students. Indeed, I would suggest that doing is much more powerful than being told, in changing attitudes and allowing enlightened insight into the issue that is being addressed.

The second issue is that of collegiality, translated in this instance into the need to respect the individual in an experiential learning environment that is high risk for both you and them. The high risk in the case of this workshop was the possibility of resentment and non-cooperation from staff who may have felt compelled to attend the workshop for political reasons associated with the arrival of a new professor rather than for intrinsic interest in the topic itself. You cannot ask staff to take on or simulate, say, the student role – in this case to undertake a test in exam conditions – unless they feel comfortable with you; unless they trust you not to make them feel foolish. By the same token, I respect the right of an individual not to take part in an exercise I am conducting. It is my job to create the climate that encourages participation, but in the end the individuals must take responsibility for their own learning. As staff development workshops are usually attended by people who are there voluntarily and who are interested in the message, it is quite unlikely that you will have non-participants, if you can meet their needs for comfort and trust.

One important aspect of trust and comfort is anonymity in a potentially risky exercise. Staff did the MCQ test anonymously, and I collated the result sheets. I think this is very important, as no one wants to be made to look silly if their results are publicly identified as outliers. (For the same reason I do not ask staff to declare their results in any classroom exercise they undertake – I simply ask them to reflect on their own results in light of the discussion about outcomes.)

The third issue is quite simple – there is no reason why staff development activities should not be fun, as well as interesting and instructive. I don't mean that they should be trivial, rather that they should be memorable for both their content and atmosphere.

The next issue is the tricky one of how you get the final message understood and embedded if you believe, as I do, that telling them is not the most effective way to do it. Experiential learning will get to the Aha! insight, as it did in this workshop, but the developer is often itching to follow this up with explicit conclusions that pull things together, and reiterate and inculcate the message. In one sense of course you must see that this happens in your session, but these are intelligent people we are working with, and they will come to sensible conclusions if given the appropriate environment in which to reflect on and discuss their workshop experiences. Some drawing together at the end of a session is usually appropriate, but I think it is much better if this final recap is made on the basis of the participants' insights rather than your own grand plan for their learning.

The final issue is the use of jargon. I have always found fellow academics very hostile to the use of educational jargon, while being not one whit bothered by their own use of jargon from their discipline. As a result, if technical language is absolutely essential to the discourse in a workshop, like the distinction between norm-referenced and criterion-referenced assessment, then I explain it as clearly as possible at the beginning of the session or section. Otherwise, I try not to use educational jargon until I am summing up or otherwise concluding a workshop session. It is quite possible to discuss assessment for formative and summative purposes, or issues of validity and reliability, without using these terms at all.

Reference

Bloom, B *et al* (1956) *Taxonomy of Educational Objectives: Cognitive Domain*, McKay, New York

SECTION 2

UNUSUAL SOURCES OF STAFF AND EDUCATIONAL DEVELOPMENT

CHAPTER 6

THE PROOF OF THE PUDDING...

Case reporter: Glenda Crosling

Issue raised

The issue raised by this case is the attitude of academic staff to faculty-based academic support for students.

Background

The case occurred in a business faculty of a large multi-campus university in Australia. The campus was the original university before amalgamations with a number of colleges of advanced education. The author had been assigned to a faculty on the original university campus after working in academic support on another campus.

PART 1

'They don't like people without PhDs at Greenfields.' These words rang in my ears as I thought about my new position. They came from a Greenfields colleague. A review of academic support had just recommended that the services our academic support unit offered on one campus, where I'd been working happily for years, were to be expanded to the other campuses of the university, including Greenfields. Greenfields was the original and largest campus of the university and, according to the new plan, academic support staff were to be located in the faculties there.

This all seemed like a very sensible arrangement to me. I'd done a lot of work integrating academic skills programmes with subject content, and I knew that it was the best way to meet students' learning needs. No doubt this experience rendered me as a suitable person for the position in the business faculty at Greenfields. Although I didn't have a PhD, I did have a Master's in applied linguistics, a strong teaching background across several educational sectors, and extensive experience in academic support. So although I felt a little disconcerted by what I had heard, I was comforted by the strength of my experience.

'They're not really interested in academic support on that campus,' said one of my colleagues, picking up on the rumours that were circulating after the review and restructure. Optimistically, I assumed that this was because they didn't really know what academic support was. I did know that some of the students needed academic support. From time to time, I'd seen students from Greenfields who made the 17 kilometre journey to the Cityview campus to get help. These were not only international students; they included a fair sprinkling of local English-speaking-background students. They needed help with academic skills in the same way as the students at Cityview.

But the staff at Greenfields, according to the people I spoke to, didn't seem to see the need for academic skills development. Their view appeared to be that if students needed assistance with their study approaches, they shouldn't be at university in the first place. I had encountered views like this at Cityview too, and knew that they didn't take account of changes that had taken place in higher education. Classes were now large. There were marked changes in the backgrounds of students enrolling, and they often needed assistance to understand academic requirements. Clearly, there would be the need for change in the attitudes of staff before they could begin to benefit from the academic support programme.

I knew that staff in the faculty at Greenfields couldn't have anything against me personally, as I had never worked there. They simply wouldn't know me. But I still felt disturbed. 'Oh well', I thought, 'I'll just have to do my best. Nobody can do more than that.'

How could I convince the staff that academic support was not spoon-feeding and that it would not compromise their high academic standards? How could I show them that students' teaching and learning needs had changed, that students from non-English-speaking backgrounds, international students, those mature in age and part timers bring to their learning a diversity that can enrich the learning of all, if we help them understand academic assumptions and expectations? It was my job, and I had to find a way for it to work.

What would you do in this situation?
Why are some academic staff reluctant to embrace academic support for students?
What do you think happened?

PART 2

The arrangement was for me to liaise with the associate dean of under-graduate teaching on the new campus. She was very supportive and encouraging, and made arrangements for me to present briefly at the new students' orientation the following week, when the dean and other faculty academic officials addressed the students. Thankfully, my short presentation went well and got the thumbs up from both the dean and the associate dean. One of the first year subject leaders approached me afterwards. 'I noticed that you mentioned analytical skills in your presentation,' he said. 'Our students need to be more analytical in approach. Can you help?' I said I could and we arranged to meet later in the semester. Things had gotten off to a good start; we were on the move and I was feeling good.

The next week, my meeting with the faculty campus course coordinator gave me an inkling of the consternation surrounding the introduction of my academic support programme in the faculty. 'We don't want you to have individual consultations with students on their unsubmitted assignments,' he told me directly. 'We need to be sure that it's the students' own work, and also it's simply not possible to offer this for all students.' He was direct, but I thought he was honest. I was comfortable with his style. So we discussed a class-based programme, and individual work for at-risk students, and I went away happy with this plan.

However, in the tearoom where the more senior staff met, I detected a somewhat ambivalent feeling about academic support. I could see that a loud 'I have all the answers' approach on my part would not go down well. Although I didn't ponder it for long (too many other things to do!), at the back of my mind I knew that there was a need to change some basic attitudes towards students and their learning. 'But how can I do that?' I thought. 'I'm not a staff developer.'

I focused on providing an integrated language and academic skills programme for students in their learning. I started working in a quiet way that suited me best. My low-key approach was based on doing rather than talking too much, and on respecting the experience and competence of academics in their own fields. This wasn't too hard because it was clear to me just how accomplished they were, and how much they cared about standards. The approach also fitted in well with what I'd learned over my years in academic support: a diplomatic approach is best when working with subject teachers. I felt intuitively that this would not threaten the assumptions of the staff about their academic programme. I also genuinely like people, and enjoy working with them, and this all helped. I hadn't read up on any theory, but based my approach on what I sensed would be the best way to go.

Things were slow to begin with. One day, just as I was thinking, 'Why aren't the staff approaching me about programmes to assist their students?', the phone rang. It was the lecturer from first-year management. 'Can you help us with our students?' he asked. 'It will mean developing a programme for the students who don't do well in the first assignment, so we'll need a series of classes, over a few weeks. I don't know if you'll have time for that…?' I was delighted! Here at last was someone taking my work seriously. And this was just the beginning of many programmes for assignments across the first-year subjects. I became very busy, and as time went on I got to know staff. I could contact them if I had several of their students coming for help, and suggest a class programme.

In retrospect, I think that just getting down and doing the job with subject staff was a good approach. Through sharing our expertise, I learnt more about the subjects and their requirements, and the staff learnt more about their students' backgrounds and how they were responding to the teaching and learning in the subject. I acted as an interpreter between the students and the subject, translating requirements and approaches for them to use in their study. I must say, though, that I did feel unnerved when subject teachers suddenly appeared to 'look in on' a class. Still, they seemed pleased with how I was working with their students, and probably just needed to feel that their students were 'safe' and I wasn't misleading them.

As time passed, I could see that the subject staff appreciated what the academic skills programme was doing for their students. I felt a sense of support from working with them, probably because I realized that they valued my work. I think that they also felt supported in our relationships. Another source of sustenance for me was my relationships with academic support staff in other faculties. We'd get together from time to time and discuss how things were going. We were not alone in our endeavours!

With even more time, faculty subject staff and I began working as teams in a true sense. We designed and presented programmes together, either in lectures, or as separate seminars. I also noticed that teachers were incorporating some of the teaching and learning ideas we discussed in their lectures and tutorials. For me, this was the highest form of achievement for my work. They were taking student learning issues seriously and addressing them!

But how could I change the attitudes of the more senior staff who ultimately make the decisions? The associate dean was very helpful with this. When I produced materials for students, she suggested I send copies to heads of departments. When I held programmes, she suggested memos about them to the heads. However, another of her suggestions had the most effect. She arranged for the assessment grades of students who had been attending my management programme to be analysed. All the same, I was a little concerned. What if the results for these students weren't good? Would this justify the views of the staff that academic support wasn't needed? Also, we know that learning is developmental, and that improvements occur on many levels, and may not immediately be realized in students' grades. I crossed my fingers and waited.

I needn't have worried. The analysis showed that the students receiving support had actually improved more than those who had not attended. The associate dean wrote an account of the analysis for the faculty newsletter. She also listed some of my recent publications on student learning in refereed journals. 'I may not have a PhD yet,' I thought, 'but I do publish in scholarly journals!'

Overall, it was a rough and in many ways difficult first year. I was constantly developing new material for my classes and, at the same time, getting to know the staff and the faculty subjects. But there did seem to be a change of attitude. Academic support was increasingly thought of as a regular feature of the faculty offerings, and I was invited to work more and more with staff. After another year, I was even granted faculty funds to investigate a student learning issue with a faculty academic. I can't think of a higher form of acceptance than that!

What do you think would have been the reaction to an advisory rather than 'hands on' approach in the faculty?
What other ways do you think could have been used to change the attitudes of staff to academic support?
What would have been the benefits and disadvantages of these?

CASE REPORTER'S DISCUSSION

It is clear from this case that what was required in the faculty was change. Change was needed in terms of recognizing that the student population was both larger and more diverse, and in recognizing that doing things to assist students in their learning is not compromising academic standards. Perhaps the crux of the success was that staff perceived that there were changes in the attitudes of many students following the introduction of the academic support programme. In some ways their teaching and assessing was easier if students knew how to structure a report or how to produce an analytical and critical legal argument.

Initially, I didn't see myself as a staff developer. My conception of staff development was going along to seminars and listening (or at times taking part in activities) about the latest on teaching and learning. I benefited a lot from seminars that I had attended, but didn't see myself in the staff developer role in the faculty.

It's only when I think back that I realize I was indeed involved in a process of staff development; staff development through working with staff in situ. The beauty of this approach was that I also grew and benefited from the experience. Through talking with staff as we developed programmes, I understood at a deeper level the values and expectations of the faculty disciplines, and these I translated into programmes for the students.

Moreover, that students performed better in their studies was not the only benefit for subject staff. Over the years, several staff told me that explaining what they wanted their students to do clarified their expectations in their own minds. A little careful and diplomatic questioning from my side also helped, I don't doubt! Questions like, 'When you say you want the students to do an essay in report form, what do you think this will look like?', and 'I've had some of your students asking me what you mean by ... in the assignment task. Do you mean ... or ...?' More than once subject staff have acknowledged that things were not stated as clearly as they had thought, and clarified matters in later lectures.

If I analyse the way I operated more carefully, I can see that it advanced on two fronts. I worked in a bottom-up way, at the grass-roots level, and also at a higher level, in a top-down way. The grass-roots level was the main focus, and it allowed me to build up credibility with staff by actually developing students' abilities in my programmes in the ways that staff wanted. Further, I was working at a practical rather than theoretical level, and this was appreciated in the business faculty. The major ace in this approach was the analysis of the students' results in the management subject. It's one thing to talk about the students seeming much more settled and more confident, but it's another to demonstrate this quantitatively. We can never pin down and factor into our evaluations all the elements that may have assisted students to develop. (After all, it could have been the most conscientious students attending the programme.) However, the result did provide some tangible evidence that the programme was having an effect on student learning.

The top-down approach proceeded much more subtly. Sending materials about programmes, and booklets that encapsulated the approach, to heads of department had a role in building credibility at this level. Heads could see and evaluate the quality of the programmes I was providing for the students. The sharing of materials and information may have had the effect of making the heads feel part of the programme, and have a sense of ownership over and involvement in it.

I believe that listing my publications may have also played a role in changing attitudes to academic support. Evidence of publications in refereed journals gave credibility to me and to the academic support field. It assisted staff at this well-established and highly reputable campus in appreciating that there was academic substance underpinning the academic support field.

The outcome of my journey as the academic skills provider in this faculty is that my conceptions of staff development have changed. While I still believe that there is a place for the didactic, seminar approach, I now know that there are other ways to effect change in a university setting. Staff development and change of attitude can also be facilitated through a hands-on, working together approach, from the bottom up. In my situation in a faculty that valued academic credibility, it was supplemented by some top-down strategies that were more directly focused on influencing perceptions.

My overall conclusion is that you need to look at the particular situation and decide which staff development approach, or which combination of approaches, is likely to be most successful. I've learnt a lot through my experiences, and the joy of working and cooperating with others is a valid way of bringing about change. We develop together, truly sharing expertise for the benefits of our students.

CHAPTER 7

MAKING A DIFFERENCE

Case reporter: Joy Higgs

Issue raised

The issue raised in this case is the costs and benefits of mentoring.

Background

A female professor at a prestigious research-led university attended a Women in Leadership programme organized by the university. Over coffee she began a conversation that continued over the next two years, as she became unofficial mentor to two colleagues in her faculty. As one of the few professors in her faculty and her profession she is often asked to support people's applications for jobs or promotion.

PART 1

I remember feeling out of place on the first day of the Women in Leadership programme. I was one of only two professors enrolled, and the other one didn't turn up. Until that point I had thought of the course as leadership development, and had believed that we could all do with some development. However, most people had come to the course seeking career advancement. Less obviously, many were looking for support; a place with a blend of security, stimulus and problem solving. Over the semester, attending once a week, we went on to spend considerable time talking about the difficulties women face advancing their careers in departments where they are in the minority.

The programme attracted mainly lecturers and senior lecturers. Some of the participants identified the tendency of women to accept organizational roles (like course coordination), leaving (most of) their male colleagues free to pursue activities that would accelerate their careers (in particular research and leadership of prestigious committees). They discussed their concerns about feeling 'used', but also were unwilling to ignore students who needed administrative support. Others raised the difficulties they faced as mothers of young children or as single parents, coping with child care responsibilities as well as trying to find enough energy and time to pursue professional and career development.

In essence, it seemed as if there was a healthy 'boys' club' and 'researchers' network' operating, but that the system did not provide career support for the people (often, but not always, women) who did not belong to these groups. And there were far fewer senior-level academic women who could serve as role models or mentors for people in this group. On one occasion a speaker from another university talked to us about strategies for developing informal support networks and about working with the people we had met at the course to support and mentor each other. And since I had more experience than most, including experience in staff selection, development and career advising, people started to ask my advice about their career advancement. Remembering the support I'd had from mentors over the years, it seemed an appropriate time for taking on the role myself.

Now all of this sounded fine in principle, and during informal discussions the mentoring task appeared neither onerous nor particularly involving. All of that changed, however, when the task became attached to particular people and their lives. Suddenly the question changed from 'Why not?' to 'What do I really know about how the system works?' and 'How can I best help them – considering there will be real consequences to my advice and their actions?' Then there are all the questions they have to face, in relation to promotion applications. For instance, is the (considerable) time involved in preparing the application worthwhile? Is promotion an option for everyone in terms of capacity to succeed and/or preparedness to try again or take a different path if unsuccessful? Is the value to the people seeking support sufficient to warrant the considerable mentoring time involved?

How would you go about mentoring if you were in the mentor's place?
Who supports or mentors the mentor?

PART 2

It was three months after the Women in Leadership programme. 'Joy, can I talk with you about applying for promotion to associate professor?' I responded to this request with a sense of pleasure and anticipation. I had worked with

Margaret for some years and saw this as a positive move. Knowing how well she was performing as a senior lecturer I saw it as a logical progression, and was confident that I could help with her preparation.

'Sure, Margaret. What's your time frame for this?' We discussed a two-year plan. This involved, first, a focus on enhancing her teaching skills by attending staff development programmes (for example, on lecturing and supervising research students). She was conducting interesting research in her speciality area and spent much time reading about the latest research in the area. We discussed ways of integrating this research into her teaching and expanding her research student supervision, with students working on projects related to her key interests. During the next year she documented these activities, conducted peer and student reviews of her teaching, and talked with me and other colleagues about how she could improve her teaching. Since her research areas and mine did not overlap I encouraged her to meet with senior researchers who could give her feedback on her research, and advise her on research directions and avenues for publications and grants. This shared mentoring was important to her but also important to me, because recognizing my lack of knowledge in her field, I wanted to avoid giving her poor advice.

Over the two-year period Margaret strengthened her knowledge and skills and broadened her perspectives as an academic. This was a rewarding time for her, and I appreciated the opportunity to help in this constructive way. Her application for promotion was excellent and we, along with other colleagues, celebrated her success. Her dual development and advancement goals worked well; and she looked back on this time and on her achievements with a real sense of accomplishment. It was the start of a pattern of development for herself and others.

'Joy, could you support my application for promotion?' It was Janice on the phone. Janice was from a different faculty, but I'd met her at the Women in Leadership course. 'I'm putting in for promotion because I've been here 10 years now, long enough service for promotion. And the work I do with my professional association is really important.'

My brain raced into gear. 'But Janice, the applications for promotion for this year have already closed. Why are you talking to me now?' After a bit of judicious questioning and discussion I found out that Janice saw promotion as a right, associated with length of service and productive work as an academic. Her standards were important to her, and she saw her goals as pre-eminent. The problem was that these goals did not coincide with the university's priorities or expectations. Nor did she consider that it was her responsibility to enhance her abilities or record in the areas which she had fewer 'runs on the board'. She had begun preparing her application just two months before the submission date. She sought support from me and from others only after submitting the application, choosing not to ask for feedback on the case she had prepared. Largely, the support requested was a token gesture. She was looking for a 'rubber stamp' from appropriately qualified senior colleagues, rather than making a genuine request for advice and mentorship.

What do you do in this position (that is, being asked to support a case you have reservations about)?
There are times when your advice or influence affects other people's lives and careers, either intentionally or unintentionally. How can you try to ensure that your advice is well-intentioned and beneficial?

PART 3

This was a difficult experience for everyone, and Janice didn't get her promotion. Mentoring, I found, can be offered, can even be unhelpful or badly directed, and in may ways can be ineffective on the part of the mentor. However, mentees also need to play their part; at the very least they need to be willing to listen with an open mind (before rejecting or accepting the advice).

I think of the next part of the case story as 'branching out', first because my mentoring role spread to a broader group than the initial group of women, and second because a number of the early group I had mentored went on to become mentors themselves.

Let me tell you the stories of Patrick and Eric. Patrick was one of the 'old school' of staff. He came to the university with a professional background, and had a strong commitment to quality teaching and to the management and development of sound curricula. As time permitted and the climate of the institution changed, he developed a solid research base. Then, enter the high flyers, the researchers and winners of very public success in 'the areas that count'. Time and again Patrick took on the administration roles, at the cost of the development of his own CV, so that others could concentrate on their research. We discussed, in the preparation of his case for promotion, the cost of these administration activities and the rewards of satisfaction in serving the needs of the students. Mentoring here was more of an affirmation of choices made, and offering recognition of his valuable supportive role, rather than being able to help him achieve success in promotion. His application for promotion was unsupported by the university, but his work was meaningful. We discussed the experience later: 'I guess we both knew that the committee wanted research – but it's really bad luck that they didn't consider all your service to the uni more fully. How are you feeling about it all?'

'Resigned, I guess. I gave it my best shot – but I'm not going to put myself through all this again... I'll just get on with the job and leave the promotions to other people. It's good to know that you and my head of school recognize my contributions. Thanks for the support. It was worth a try, I suppose.'

On the other hand, from the start of his career, Eric seemed blessed with a clear understanding of what 'the system' wanted. He taught well, contributed to decision-making committees, finished his PhD in record time and rapidly produced a long list of publications and grants. We talked from time to time about career progression, looking at achieving a balance of contributions across teaching, research, administration and leadership, and identifying strategic moves to prepare his case for promotion to one level and then another. His case was strong and his success was straightforward. Interestingly, his need for mentoring, apart from the strategizing, was to receive recognition for the valuable contributions he was making. He commented, 'I was really pleased to get such positive feedback on my people skills. I like to think I get along with people well – it's more important to me in many ways than my academic achievements.' Acknowledgement of his humanity rather than his ambition was rewarding for him. He'll make a great all-round leader in the near future.

And what happened to Margaret and Janice? Well, Janice is still ranting about the injustices of the system. She wants the rules changed to suit what she thinks she should be doing, rather than what the collective mind of the university (or at least the principal decision makers with some input from the masses) considers is required for advancement. She's chosen not to seek promotion again. From time to time our paths cross at university events. She continues to go her own way.

Margaret and I continue to work together from time to time in interdepartmental projects. Occasionally she seeks my advice, but largely we've moved on to a new peer relationship. She has herself become a mentor to others. She participates in the orientation of new staff, advising them on their professional development and promotion prospects and helping with specific advice (such as research methodology) in her areas of strength. Since her promotion she has expanded her leadership roles and influence at department, faculty and university level. Her professional development is a good example of broadening and deepening her academic competencies and productivity, of balancing self-advancement with service, and of integrating the privilege of senior rank with the responsibilities that go with it.

Consider the role of the mentor in 'letting go' and enabling the (former) mentee in turn to become a mentor. How can mentors move on from the mentor role to the colleague or partner role?
What strategies could be used to help people feel self-worth if the system does not recognize them through reward systems (eg, promotion)?
What networks or support systems have you set up to help yourself face the challenges of academic life?

CASE REPORTER'S DISCUSSION

The rewards of mentoring can be numerous. Helping others achieve their goals is satisfying, as is seeing people move beyond their current aspirations, to be better teachers or researchers, to take on new challenges and to gain greater job fulfilment. It's a good feeling to actually do yourself out of the job of mentoring as your mentee grows beyond your advice, to gain a colleague and someone who in turn helps to stretch you. To see people achieve and to know you have helped in some way makes the endeavour of mentoring very worthwhile.

The dilemmas of mentoring cannot be so easily summed up. Sometimes you can ask yourself – what's the difference between interference and assistance, between support and direction, between guidance and constraint? Finding the balance between these polarities also leads to the question – do I really know how best to advise this person, or is someone else better for the job? In some respects, being part of the academic leadership brings considerable experience of assessing issues of quality through participating in selection and promotion committees, reviewing applications and acting as referee. Through such activities and through collaboration in policy design and academic standards discussions, you gain an idea of the expectations facing academic staff in their work and their promotion or appointment applications. Yet it is valuable to retain a healthy degree of self-doubt and humility in this challenging task. You don't want to steer people in the wrong direction.

In juggling our workloads as academics there are times when we have to reflect on the cost to self of other people's needs, development and time pressures. The mentor as well as the mentee needs to pace workload demands. One of the best pieces of advice I've been given (and passed on to others) is to prepare early for major events such as interviews, applications and presentations. This gives more time for practice and feedback, and reduces last-minute stress. It also helps if mentors have a reasonable timeframe to read long documents like applications and teaching portfolios, and find time to slot this task in with existing workloads. Sometimes, in self-preservation, it may be necessary to ask your colleague to pass the review task on to someone else. Of course, this is easier said than done! There are times when you know how much pressure your colleague is under preparing for the application, and you don't want to let him or her down, but you're simply drowning in work yourself – so you somehow find the time.

Another dilemma mentors face arises when they perceive the need to discourage a colleague from seeking promotion, an appointment or a desired position (such as chair of a committee). This is a difficult job. You somehow need to balance affirmation of them as a person with talking them into delaying or passing up a career opportunity. There are situations when you consider that people need more experience, stronger grounds in support of their case, or more time to choose their direction. Sometimes, based on your experience, you may even consider that they do not meet the criteria, or that the direction they're contemplating has more disadvantages than advantages. How sure are you in giving this advice? What will be the consequences for the person? What is the cost to you of this decision – did you give good advice? How can you deal with the disappointment or even resentment of your colleague?

Is this dilemma better or worse than dealing with unsuccessful outcomes and supporting your colleague facing feelings of anger, self-doubt or regret? Perhaps it's better for them (and you?) to 'have a go' and take a risk. Talking through the options, giving your reasoned opinions, and encouraging them to consult with others helps to deal with this issue.

A key strategy in mentoring is listening and finding out what your colleagues want or hope to do. Talking through the options and seeing what they think about the various choices is invaluable. Sometimes the success of professional development is not in public changes in status, position or achievements. It can be in a sense of relief, of satisfaction or validation; perhaps in affirmation of a decision not to change the current position, or in encouragement to try out some new teaching approach or research endeavour instead. Mentoring doesn't have to be visible or publicly acknowledged to be of real benefit to both parties. In the highly competitive world of academia there is still a place for actions that have value, even if they don't accrue public reward.

Such individual action of support is a small part of the informal network of mentoring and collegiality that exists in most tertiary education systems. New colleagues are welcomed and inducted into the system, peer support is provided to people facing life or curricular challenges, and collegial support for many people is a way of life in academia. As a result of the women's leadership programme, a university network of women was established to provide informal support and mentoring of staff wanting to engage in professional development and seek promotion. This support is not limited to women, but often seeks to address the imbalance in the ratio of senior appointments and promotions for women compared with men. These informal strategies (sustained by the largely invisible and unrecognized work of staff acting as in-service organizers and mentors) form the backbone of staff development alongside more organized systems such as seminars, workshops and university-funded staff training programmes (such as teacher training, development of research and supervision skills, and acquisition of knowledge and skills in areas of university system management such as staff appraisal and financial management).

One such programme I helped to initiate involved the organization, at a faculty level, of promotion seminars to help people recognize the nature and extent of the task of preparing for promotion. The seminars covered strategies for pursuing and recording professional development and career activities that are needed to develop 'the substance' or the grounds for promotion, understanding the requirements for promotion from the perspective of the different levels of committees that consider the application, and preparation of the case or argument in support of their application. After two years of my organizing these seminars they became an institutional activity with central organization. On an individual level I discussed people's draft applications, their aspirations and the work needed to make a solid case.

Overall, mentoring plays an important role in systems and staff development. Systems and people place considerable demands and expectations on experienced and senior academics, particularly women, to provide support for colleagues. Greater support for and recognition of mentoring is needed to sustain this valuable staff development activity. For mentors themselves, it's important to find a balance between the rewards, costs and dilemmas of mentoring. To fulfil this role there is a need for informal networks as well as personal support to supplement organized staff development programmes.

Questions for personal reflection

- What is your own experience of being mentored?
- What does it take to be an effective mentor?

CHAPTER 8

Walking a Tightrope

Case reporter: Carmel McNaught

Issue raised

This case raises the issue of how a staff development unit can react when the university administration demands evidence of outcomes related to strategic goals and the financial implications thereof.

Background

A large 'corporate' university in Australia has a considerable investment in IT infrastructure and associated staff development. In the process of the IT implementation, the staff development unit has built up good relationships with faculty staff.

PART 1

'They want us to … what?' I spluttered. I had dropped into my director's office as I usually did on a Wednesday to touch base and catch up. Casually, towards the end of our 15-minute conversation, he showed me the minutes of the committee that managed investment in IT. The university, it seemed, wanted evidence that it was likely to get a return on its investment.

We all know times are fraught in universities: increased pace of change, increasing diversity in the student population, really serious funding cuts. The cry is 'build more business', increase the number of international students, become competitive. All universities are investing heavily in IT systems and services to assist in streamlining operations and easing the funding crisis. Ours was no exception.

As a staff development unit, we had been involved in our university's substantial investment into the use of technology in several areas in infrastructure, enterprise computer-based systems, digital library resources and staff development. While the overall balance was fairly good there were lots of hiccups (well, let's be honest, more like paroxysms) during implementation of the technical systems, but a sense that this was the right approach still prevailed.

The teaching and learning arena in our university is complex. There is a wide variation in the programme and course designs used across the university. Most courses are not fully online and involve mixed-mode designs including traditional classroom face to face teaching, workplace learning arrangements and partnerships with other educational providers (especially offshore). Huge changes in a short period of time sent stress levels soaring, and tolerance levels plummeting. Many academics found the increasing emphasis on the use of computer technology for administration, research and teaching highly threatening. And it wasn't just the technology. The associated changes in academic work practices were hard for many to accept and use.

We in the staff development unit knew about these fears, and knew we needed to focus on building staff confidence and motivation as well as providing adequate support and training opportunities. We had already run discussion sessions about flexible learning and the potential role of technology in all the faculties and in several of the departments. We had lots of conversations about needs and challenges. We had heard and seen the huge diversity in culture and local support for the use of technology across this very large university.

We had listened to academic teachers talk about the hurdles and dilemmas that they had to negotiate, some of which were:

- If I 'go online', what does this mean to my role as a teacher?
- Will I be flooded with e-mail messages?
- How do I cope with the copyright maze? What is happening to my intellectual property? What rights do I have to use resources I find on the Web?
- How many more times will the system crash? Will they (never named) ever get this system stable?
- How can I check on whether my students are coping with all this? Do they have access?
- Does all this really help my students learn?

So how did we go about trying to assist this process of change?

We mounted a large-scale professional development exercise that involved time release (26 days for most people; some had even longer periods of time), training and ongoing support for approximately 145 staff across the university. Two or three academic staff in each department of the university participated in the programme. They went to about five days of workshops and training in total, developed online materials, and worked with their colleagues in their departments on small online teaching and learning projects.

This time was a real high point. The engagement of the participants in workshops and their appreciation of the time release were both great. The sessions covered the usual range of topics: practical 'hands-on' online tools training sessions, as well as workshops in areas such as course design, assessment and evaluation strategies for online learning, student induction methods, finding and managing digital resources, project management, copyright, publishing standards and so on. But the difference was that our participants had definite goals and some time available to try to achieve them. We also spent a great deal of time answering queries and providing advice to individuals. This could be quite difficult and intense when the online learning system was going through yet another period of instability after some technical upgrade or 'tweaking' had occurred.

After all this effort a really nice period emerged. The system stabilized, confidence was increasing, the first plateau of ease arrived. There were several hundred online courses, and many teachers were seriously tackling issues about how best to design online learning environments.

I should have known it wouldn't last! As the director casually showed me the brief section of the minutes of the university committee that managed the investment in IT that morning, a great sinking feeling began. The gist of the minute was that the university wanted evidence that it was likely to get a return on its investment:

- Were our online courses worth the money?
- Had we improved our marketability in the international arena?
- Did the university have clear organizational control over its online courses?

The mandated strategy for answering these questions was that of an external audit with the central support unit (us!) acting as judge on whether each online course was sufficiently developed and 'correctly' designed.

A mandated audit flew in the face of so many of the principles of collegial, evolutionary development that had guided our work to this point. We were in quite a dilemma, and the crisis seemed so unnecessary. But what should we do?

What options are available to the staff development unit?
What do you think will happen next?
Have you considered similar 'audit' versus 'development' tensions and if so, how were they resolved?

PART 2

At this stage we had new courseware being largely developed within the corporate online learning system, but also there was a significant amount of online courseware residing on departmental and faculty servers. The central audit team was directed to identify and audit this non-centrally located 'feral' courseware and organize its migration to a central server. I, as head of the central professional development unit, was to manage this audit and provide a judgement on each online course.

'My role is not a police role,' said Anne.

'Just how many hours will it take for us to look at all the online courses?' asked John.

'Well, it's just not possible!' said Denise.

'And how boring!' sighed Roland.

These were some of the comments (actually expressed with somewhat more invective) that poured out when our small group of staff developers got together later that morning. But we were all seasoned campaigners in staff development, and the phase of anger and denial was relatively short. It was surprisingly easy to reach a decision about the strategy we would adopt. Compliance was simply not an option; it just went too much against the grain. Defiance would just mean that an external auditor would be brought in (we'd seen that happen to others before) and we would have no say in the process. I'm not sure we saw ourselves instantly as active subversive agents (attractive though the image is). We had decided not to comply or defy. We knew that some strategy was needed that would result in some evaluative comments being made about all the online courses. A collaborative approach with faculties was a natural solution. This fitted with the approach we had taken all along, and pragmatically meant that there would be more people to do the work. It was only later that we came to view this as a subversive path.

We used four main strategies, namely the careful use of terminology, appropriate selection of teams, identifying achievable outcomes, and downplaying problematic issues at the beginning.

Careful use of terminology

The word 'audit' was simply not used by me or any of the staff in the central unit. We used the word 'review'. When we were speaking to or writing to our faculty colleagues, we spoke about the 'collaborative review' and framed goals such as 'giving course owners collective feedback to assist them in further development'. When we were speaking to or writing to staff in the university administration, we described forming 'review teams with an appropriate breadth of discipline and pedagogical expertise' and described our work as leading to 'detailed and informed data on online courses'.

Appropriate selection of teams

It is hard to change an organizational structure once it is in place, and so sometimes it is wiser not to seek approval for changing a project's methodology. We simply approached colleagues in faculty roles, explained the university's request for a clear picture of the current state of online learning in the university, and suggested that we could achieve that purpose while also giving useful evaluative feedback to the staff who had invested quite a deal of effort into developing some online component of their courses. The teams consisted of members from the central unit who were all experienced staff developers/educational designers, and staff from the faculties who were experienced online teachers and who understood more about faculty programmes and discipline areas than we did.

We proposed collaborative teams, and the teams were in place before the difference between this collaborative strategy and an external audit by the central unit alone was noticed. When this difference was noticed, the explanation was given that the review would obtain more accurate information if we had input about the nature of the discipline areas in each faculty, and the overall structure of the programmes in which this online courseware was situated. We also pointed out quite clearly that the workload involved in a university-wide review meant that we needed to share the load with faculty colleagues. There was no objection.

Identification of achievable outcomes

The first review I was involved in recognized that an academic teacher in a department can be far removed from the reality of central university administration. We had many staff who wanted to get involved in understanding online teaching and learning, but it wasn't an assigned professional role and was not of high priority to them. Such teachers might do a little training and come to a workshop or two, set up a course site, and add a few bits and pieces to it, before being overwhelmed by other pressures. Objectively, the sites they created were not high-quality online sites, but to remove them would cut off the possibilities of growth for the future. So we developed strategies for diplomatic feedback in the first review. If a site was actually empty, we asked that it not be 'live' to students until it was developed. If the site was very embryonic, we suggested the same. Each site therefore remained waiting until the teacher concerned had time and energy to develop it into a resource that would be of value to students.

This first review fed into the formulation of a process for allowing students access to a course site. This process became part of the university's quality assurance policy. Any staff member could have a course site but it could only become 'live' to students if it had undergone some scrutiny and seemed to be a coherent resource. For most courses this sign-off occurred at faculty level. A sign-off on copyright clearance was also included.

In the second review, a year later, we used a negotiated pro forma (see Figure 8.1) in order to get a clearer picture about how staff actually used the functions of online technology. This asked for information about the course and then provided a checklist related to the functions of online design, a modified version of which is below. Again, we used collaborative central–faculty teams, and all the review team had to do was indicate which functions were seen in the course site under review. In many cases, though, comments were also made.

Figure 8.1   Sample pro forma

Section A: Educational planning and design of online environments	
Topic	**Some examples to consider**
Learner–learner/learner–teacher interaction	• Online tutorial sessions. • Feedback on practical work. • Continuous evaluation form. • Team assignments workspace. • Moderated discussion forums.
Learner self-assessment/feedback on learning progress	• A current collection of assessment materials and supporting documentation. • Samples of previous assignments/project work (with documented student permission). • A collection of past/recent exams and sample tests (where appropriate). • Self-help quizzes (for formative assessment purposes). Provision for electronic submission of assignment work. Publishing work for peer review.
Study programme management/study skills support	• Direct access to the related approved course guide. • A current timetable/timeline related to outlining face to face tutorials, lectures, lab/field work and online activities (with times, dates and location details). Online learning activities clearly described/linked to curriculum outcomes. • Current contact details of lecturers, teachers and tutors. A structured collection of Frequently Asked Questions and/or Glossary. • Lecture outlines. • Laboratory notes. • News announcements.
Resource-based/problem-based learning environments	• A structured collection of learning resources. • Clear links to related library resources and databases. A structured and validated collection of annotated WWW links. • Multimedia simulations.

Downplaying problematic issues at the beginning

At the beginning we had no idea how to handle the vexed issue of 'feral' courseware. Indeed, we did not think this was the main priority at the time. While there is a clear technical argument for having all courseware on corporate servers which are well serviced and of a high standard, one doesn't do much for academic morale if files are transferred without careful negotiation with the people who invested a great deal of time and effort into their development and who feel they 'own' them. At the time of the first review, the university's online system had not been a stable platform for long, and the performance from faculty servers was actually often better. Persuading academics to make a change that does not have clearly demonstrable benefits is just not sensible. It turned out that our intuition was correct. By the time we got to the second review, the university's platform was regarded as reliable and the matter was seen in a different light. Many staff had set up sites in the online system to take advantage of online forums or quiz facilities. They just added links to their other sites, so the issue of migration became one of just being technically tidy.

What elements of the approach taken led to a positive conclusion?
What other approaches could have been taken and what would have been the likely outcomes?

CASE REPORTER'S DISCUSSION

This case is about strategies for managing change. Some of the key issues for staff development units in managing change are:

- adhering to established principles;
- dealing with the emotional aspects of change;
- finding the middle ground;
- using reflection to enable growth.

Adhering to established principles

It was not at all difficult to reach our decision. Just accepting an edict that seemed to be counter-productive to the long-term goals of the whole investment strategy wasn't an option. As a group, the staff developers were quite clear that we operated through the use of collegial processes. We also accepted that meaningful change takes time. Long-term change is evolutionary, not revolutionary.

Unless one believes in an evolutionary approach, the slow pace of progress can be daunting and disheartening. When we began the first review, I must confess to having a sinking feeling at seeing so many empty or minimal sites. Such sites do not represent a 'return on investment'. How can we support staff in this situation? Being able to portray the first review as an opportunity to ensure that students would have access to high-quality (well, at least coherent) sites, as well as maintaining the momentum (albeit low) of other staff, was an achievement. We were able to portray the review as a step forward.

The subversive art here is to design a project methodology that will allow the work to be done most effectively; justifying sensible decisions after the event is not difficult.

Dealing with the emotional aspects of change

How did we, as a staff development unit, feel about this threat to the investment we had so carefully made to building up productive working relationships, especially as we knew that these relationships were still fragile in some cases? There was anger and frustration in the team that needed to be talked through. Sure, staff development is not as fraught as being in an emergency room in a hospital, but we were feeling that the vagaries of the technology had put us (as well as the staff we work with) under considerable pressure. We had to manage our own fatigue and frustration, as well as maintain support for those we work with. Changing educational practices and styles can produce many negative reactions, and this negativity needs to be acknowledged and managed effectively, both within staff development units and in working with teaching colleagues.

Finding the middle ground

Instead of thinking of a range of problems, issues or options that needs to be considered during the implementation of an innovation, Johnson (1992) suggests that it is more realistic to consider a series of polarities. He claims that polarities are sets of opposites that can't function well independently. Because the two sides of a polarity are interdependent, it is not possible to choose one as a solution and neglect the other. The aim of polarity management is to get the best of both opposites while avoiding the limits of each. The solution resides within the tension between polarities. For example, we can view collaboration and competition as being at two poles; they are not mutually exclusive, but rather both need to be accommodated in our strategic planning. Polarity theory does not offer defined solutions to organizational problems. It emphasizes that change is messy and dynamic; as the appropriate balance point for one set of polarities shifts, this will influence others. I have found ideas such as those Johnson articulates really helpful. There are always some valid points for each side of an argument (even though this may be difficult at the time!). In this case, both perspectives are correct. Central units have obligations to support staff in faculties, and also have an obligation to provide university administration with as accurate a picture as possible about the successes and challenges of work at faculty level. We have to walk a tightrope and serve two masters.

There is always a middle ground where this can be done. We have already said that compliance was too contrary to the principles the staff development group adhered to. Defiance was also not seen as an option, as the risks associated with allowing a group without an academic focus to manage the audit seemed to us to be just too great. Anyway, defiance is not often a viable option. It is usually seen as naïve and inappropriate in senior academic circles. We were naturally drawn to the middle ground – active but subtle subversion was an appealing challenge!

Part of the art of being subversive is judging the best time to tackle issues. Often imperatives from above come with a return date of yesterday, but often it is possible to tackle urgent matters and recognize when other issues can wait. There is always a middle ground.

Using reflection to enable growth

I have been in staff development now for over 10 years and have worked in four very different universities in that time – a rich tapestry of experience. After each major challenge, there is always an opportunity for growth. This particular experience clarified for me the three points I have made above. It gave me confidence that solutions do exist for the constant barrage of dilemmas. And it is this optimistic message I would like to share with other staff developers who are constantly teetering on one tightrope or another.

In recent years staff developers working in IT areas may have felt under particular pressure because there have been many stressful implementations of enterprise computer systems. There is also the issue that electronic courseware can be considered an object and become the locus for a control and ownership issue. Hopefully, the issues of technical stability will improve and intellectual property will be something that is negotiated easily. Yes, I am Pollyanna, but otherwise I would have ulcers!

Reference

Johnson, B (1992) *Polarity Management: Identifying and managing unsolvable problems*, HRD Press, Amherst, MA

CHAPTER 9

By accident or...?

Case reporter: David Murphy

Issue raised

The issue raised in this case is the need to be alert for staff development opportunities that may arise from unexpected or unanticipated sources.

Background

The case explores the development and presentation of an online course offered by a distance teaching university. The non-credit course, Mining Information in the Internet Age, was developed for a continuing education division, and was designed to improve participants' skills at finding, evaluating and using information from the Internet. It also provided access to the university's electronic library, and included material and exercises designed to ensure that users were able to make maximum use of electronic resources. The case reporter was the writer of the course, supported by a team of academic and library staff.

PART 1

I like my work. I've been involved in distance and open learning for many years, and have enjoyed working in a variety of institutions, watching and being a part of ongoing developments in the field. Course design and development is a great field to be part of, especially with all the new and emerging technologies that are enabling us to try out new ways of doing things. That is my basic responsibility as leader of a small group of course designers, though the unit I am a member of also provides general educational technology services, and has responsibility for aspects of staff development such as training for the institution's large number of part-time tutors. So my job is varied and challenging, enabling me to take part in all sorts of interesting projects across the curriculum, and providing the opportunity to interact with differing groups of staff. And so it was that my head of department handed me the responsibility for something new, a short online course for our continuing education institute.

It was a fun project. There I was, keen to extend my skills at online course development, given the opportunity for relative freedom in designing and developing a 'purely' online course. Because it was non-credit bearing, there were fewer of the restrictions that can impinge on one's more creative urges, and being a short course, it wouldn't become a burdensome task. As a team, we could have contracted an outside writer, but members were happy enough to give me a go at it when I volunteered. It seemed that we had the expertise and resources internally, and that it would take considerable time and effort to 'train someone up' in what we wanted. So away we went, embarking on a development schedule that took nearly six months.

As Mining Information in the Internet Age is essentially about improving information literacy skills, I spent some time gathering online resources from the wealth of available relevant sites. These not only provided me with plenty of links for later use, but also developed my thinking about the structure of the course. This in turn helped with writing the course blueprint, a document that is circulated among relevant university staff before the course is approved for development.

I was keen that the online course should have an attractive 'look and feel'. The software that the university uses for its online courses does not have a particularly pleasant interface, but I was lucky enough to be working in a department with graphic and programming staff able to create an alternative approach. Not happy with the 'clunky' functionality and frankly boring interface of typical software, I wanted something that was more like an online newspaper. My half-baked notions and sketches were readily consumed by our accommodating senior graphic artist, who came back with a design that surpassed my expectations and delighted the course team. It was colourful, attractive and intuitive to use.

As far as structure is concerned, Mining Information in the Internet Age is divided into three units:

Unit 1: A strategy for searching for information
Unit 2: Finding information
Unit 3: Evaluating and citing information

Unit 1 presents a five-step strategy for searching for information, which seeks to answer the following questions:

1. What am I looking for?
2. Where can I look for the information?

3. How can I find the information?
4. How do I evaluate the information?
5. How can I use my information source/s?

These steps form the basis for the course content.

Participants are presented with a number of scenarios of persons seeking information from a variety of perspectives, and stages of the scenarios are integrated with the study units, culminating in final outcomes at the end of Unit 3. In addition, participants are led through a series of activities that allow them to apply the steps to their own information-searching needs. For me the activities were crucial to the success or otherwise of the course, as I wanted participants not only to rethink how they find and use information, but also to become 'critical connoisseurs' of both that information and the tools used to find it.

The features of each unit include:

- standard header with links to other units, the home page, the discussion group, etc;
- contents list on the left, with each entry linked to content page;
- right-hand side used for links to relevant external Web sites and 'extras' (extension work);
- page contents displayed dynamically (adjusts to browser settings) in the middle;
- 'previous', 'next' and 'top' buttons; and
- self-assessment activities integrated with the contents.

Multimedia elements in the course include audio introductions to each unit, and demonstrations of the use of software, developed using Camtasia (http://www.camtasia.com/). This product allows videos to be made of a computer screen, with added audio for explanation.

Unit 2 was by far the longest, with detailed information and activities related to use of the university's electronic library, along with material about search engines and information sources, including a focus on regional offerings. Unit 3 contained my pride and joy, the Quality of Information Evaluation Tool (QuIET), which participants applied in an interactive activity that required them to evaluate a number of Web sites and compare their findings with others' results. It also included material and a number of links on plagiarism (and how to avoid it, of course!).

Although the course was, I thought, suitable for wholly independent study, team members were keen to incorporate opportunities for interaction among participants, and so a discussion group was incorporated into the online learning environment. At various strategic spots in the course, participants were encouraged to share their findings and questions with others through the discussion group. The tutor would also be involved, answering both academic and administrative queries.

Overall, I was pleased with and proud of the result. The course was delivered on schedule, and incorporated many of the notions I knew were required for effective online learning. This was especially true of the activities, which were interactive, challenging, and for the most part related to the interests or context of participants. I'd also been able to apply the skills I'd developed with previous online courses, and developed new skills through interaction with others involved in the development.

During the final stages of development and testing, advertising for the course began. We had high hopes of substantial numbers of people enrolling, and contacts had been made with schools and government agencies to attract staff members to the course. At the final few meetings, we would eagerly ask the continuing education representative about numbers. 'Well, it's early days yet; most enrolments usually come in at the end for this kind of course' was his initial reply. But as the starting date drew nearer, things didn't improve, so that by the close of enrolments, only 11 persons had signed up. Dismal news, indeed!

Faced with this situation what would you do?
Could anything have been done to avoid this situation?

PART 2

Normally with such small numbers, a course of this type would be cancelled. However, as it involved a minimum of face to face sessions, and I'd agreed to act as tutor (thus saving additional costs), we went ahead.

Most of the participants turned up to the initial tutorial, designed to acquaint them with the online learning environment and the essential elements of the course. Chatting with them, it soon became apparent that a few of them (school librarians) had no idea what they were enrolled for, having been 'directed' to join by their school principal. This did not necessarily make them the most eager of participants. So the course spluttered into life, and ran for the allotted schedule, with little activity on the online discussion group, despite my best efforts to arouse interest.

However, all was not lost. The course team was still having its meetings, and at one of them an alternative use of the course was suggested. I would of course like to claim that it was my bright idea, but in truth I cannot remember who came up with it. The idea was to offer the course to staff of the university. The unit I work in was already involved in staff development, particularly with the training of the large numbers of part-time tutors that the university employs, so it wasn't a foreign notion. And I had worked in an academic staff development unit at my previous university.

In fact the idea seemed eminently sensible. The university was keen to assist staff in upgrading their IT skills, and the content of the course would fit the requirements. Further, I was confident that the course would need only minor alteration to suit this potential group of learners. Thus, with the help of human resources staff, who oversee staff training, we went ahead. They were always on the lookout for new courses, so to have something ready-made and ready to go was warmly welcomed. Within a couple of months of the public offering of the course, a version was made freely available to all staff of the university.

Initial enrolments were encouraging, with 40 people signing up – quite a good number for an institution with not many more than 100 academics. This included both administrative and academic staff, and even one of the deans. Two familiarization sessions were conducted, and were well attended. These were run in a computer lab, where participants could log on, scan the course contents and post initial messages to the discussion group. This approach appeared to work well, as the discussion group was quite active over the life of the course.

Of the 40 starters, 33 completed all requirements (online tests, evaluation feedback) and were deemed to have passed the course. The three online tests were in the form of multiple-choice quizzes, which both tested participants' knowledge of the course, and required them to locate obscure pieces of information concerning Hong Kong's basic law, or from such sources as the Vatican Archives and the National Library of Canada. Three attempts at each of the quizzes (there were three versions of each for Units 2 and 3) were allowed. And as those who have developed such assessment items well know, they take ages to develop! Thankfully, participants seemed to enjoy the quizzes, especially the sometimes quirky searches that they had to complete to find the answers.

Overall, the feedback from participants was pleasingly positive, with, for example, nearly 90 per cent agreeing or strongly agreeing that they now 'have a useful strategy for locating and evaluating information'. Further, a similar percentage would recommend the course to their friends. Individual comments on what participants enjoyed about the course included:

The resources revealed; the activities and the quizzes; the great design of the site (really nicely planned out and very attractive!).

The evaluating strategy for Web information is very useful. Many useful tools and sources for searching are provided. Atomica is a very useful resource. Activities are quite interesting.

The course gives us a systematic approach of doing a search in the WWW and lots of useful tips for evaluating the information obtained. This course alerts me to important issues when doing a search on the WWW, things that I have not paid much attention to before the course.

The messages on the discussion group also included encouraging comments, one of the most pointed being:

> This online electronic course is extremely useful, convenient, resource-saving, and cost-effective. We can arrange self-study and practice systematically, step by step, activity by activity, unit by unit. The resources/Web sites available are very handy and useful.

As a result of this, the human resources unit has decided to continue to offer the course to staff, making it additionally available to part-time tutors. The pool of potential users has thus increased by over 1,000, making the initial decision to develop the course appear a good one.

CASE REPORTER'S DISCUSSION

This simple case study has highlighted the need to be alert for opportunities for staff development from unexpected sources. Universities offer a wealth of study opportunities to their students, and many of their courses can also be attractive to their staff. This is especially true for the kind of skills-based training that is currently required to bring all members of the university community 'up to speed' with advances in information technology and the use of computers. By offering them an online course, we can give a real 'hands on' feel for what it is like to be an online student. They can also glean ideas for their own courses, and become acquainted with the software that they may be required to apply in their teaching, such as the use of online discussion groups.

Online learning opportunities can be especially attractive to university staff, both academic and administrative, as this case has shown. One added benefit is the relative anonymity that individualized online instruction can offer, so that senior staff, who may be embarrassed at having to turn up to class alongside their junior colleagues, can undertake skills upgrading in the privacy of their own office.

And of course there is a multitude of other resources available from the Internet that can, when judiciously chosen, be used for staff development purposes. At the previous university in which I worked, we offered a Graduate Certificate in Higher Education to academic staff which made extensive use of links in the online component of the course. It makes simple sense that it is wasteful to develop your own materials when they may already exist in acceptable form at the click of a button. There are, for example, more than enough university Web sites that include competent outlines on the strengths and weaknesses of objectives in the planning of courses. The trick is being able to localize the resources so that they achieve your aims, and this calls for careful planning and skilled programme development.

Finally, it is also a simple issue of efficiency in the use of resources, a positive outcome for all concerned. So the lesson for us is to look out for opportunities to turning existing learning resources, prepared for students or otherwise, into suitable forms for use in staff development.

Note: A demonstration version of the course (without some features, such as the discussion group) can be viewed at http://webct.ouhk.edu.hk. Click on 'My WebCT' and log on with username 'ogus32590_h0' and password 'ouhkguest'.

SECTION 3

DRIVING CHANGE IN FACULTIES AND INSTITUTIONS

CHAPTER 10

I WILL SURVIVE

Case reporters: Robyn Lines and Peter Muir

Issues raised

The issues raised in this case are how to create a collaborative, action learning team to effect major curriculum development, together with coping with dissent at different levels.

Background

This case occurred in an Australian university during 2001. The university was redefining its strategic direction, and identified the transformation of all its degree programmes from a traditional content-based curriculum to one leading to the development of graduate capability outcomes as a key priority. The Business faculty chose a new Bachelor of Commerce as the first capability-based programme to be developed. The authors led a team made up of staff from each school that contributed to the new programme, staff from the library and other support areas and a university expert, Ian, who had contributed extensively to theorizing the idea of a capability-based curriculum. None of the team had any practical experience in designing a programme based on this innovative concept, so they decided that an action learning model provided the best approach.

PART 1

Ian, our university expert on capability-based curriculum approaches, was speaking forcefully at one of our regular team workshops. 'What you've got to understand is that what we do now is add a dose of skills development to a traditional curriculum. This is not what a capability approach is about. It won't be enough. You have to be prepared to let go and completely rethink what…'

Tony, one of the school representatives, rose from his seat and thrusting his chest forward interrupted, 'I take exception to your tone!' Ian also rose from his seat. The tension was palpable. It felt more like a fight scene from a school yard than a group of academics working collaboratively to design a new curriculum. How could it have come to this? Peter, who was leading the workshop, somehow managed to defuse the incident and bring the event to a close. We retired to debrief. What was going on here?

For some time we seemed to have been going round in circles. The members of the design team came from five disciplinary backgrounds. Each adopted an approach to curriculum design and teaching practice that reflected some fundamental differences in their understanding of how the world worked and the nature of knowledge and learning.

There was also questionable commitment to the task itself. The project had been initiated as part of university policy, and some of the team members saw it as another silly fad that, like other initiatives in the past, would go away if they just delayed long enough. Others believed that it made no sense because it was clearly impossible to build this kind of curriculum within the constraints of an under-funded university sector. Others felt that no change was necessary because they couldn't see how it differed from their current practice. We seemed to be stalemated by a range of arguments that cycled between 'It shouldn't be done', 'It can't be done' and 'We're doing it anyway'. In an effort to break the stalemate we met with all the team members individually outside the workshop sessions, but nothing seemed to have much effect.

The challenges and uncertainties of the curriculum design task were compounded by other changes that were occurring across the university. The state of constant change that characterizes the environment for Australian universities had been increased following the appointment of a new vice chancellor who had new ideas about what was important. We invested a lot of effort in talking to leaders in other sections of the university in an effort to clarify some of the issues that were inhibiting the progress of the design team. The problem was that these groups too were dealing with uncertainty and could provide no real firm ground for our work. Practically everything was uncertain.

There were two different responses to this within the team. One tendency was to try and cast us as instructors – 'It's your project so just tell us the answer and let's get on with it.' It seemed quite threatening for some members of the design team to accept that we didn't know the answer, and in fact no one could provide the answer.

The other tendency was to redefine the problem in such a way that it became a simple commercial proposition rather than a complex educational renewal project. In one memorable encounter, a team member captured the mood of a workshop when he said, 'Look, the way I've seen this all along is there is no mileage in this approach. The financial model is all screwed up. We're never going to make any money from this. We should just cut our losses, put together a group of our existing courses and be done with it.'

So looking back, it is understandable that this workshop erupted as it did. It all seemed to be just too hard. Perhaps we were too ambitious to expect the team to develop a radically new curriculum in such a complex and uncertain environment. We had certainly under-estimated the obstacles of adopting an action learning approach in such a context. Notions that by creating an open process the team would engage with the key issues and jointly discover the solution had been clearly misplaced. We had been unable to build a shared understanding of the nature of the task, and a number of boundary issues had proven to be insurmountable obstacles. As a result there had been little evidence of constructive or collaborative action emerging from the team.

Feeling rather perplexed and dispirited that the previous couple of months had resulted in little obvious progress, we decided to take stock before planning our next steps.

Do you think that there were things that could have been done to create a more productive working environment?
What do you think could be done to retrieve the situation and create the conditions to get on with the work?

PART 2

After thinking about what had happened we felt clearer, at least, about the problems we faced. More than ever we felt that we had to find ways to create conditions where team members felt safe enough to work in new and creative ways. A few things seemed clear. We both agreed that we shouldn't attempt to sweep the hostility and defensiveness under the carpet. We needed to use it as a key opportunity for learning. We might be able to use it as a vehicle for engaging the group in reflection about what was going on, and as a means of getting them to take some responsibility as a team for the future of the project.

First we needed to consolidate our own learning. Upon reflection it seemed in leading an action learning team we had taken a highly discursive approach to the initial stages. We had opened up a 'Pandora's box' of issues which may well have been relevant but which the group had no capacity to influence or control. We had tried to 'talk' our way through these issues but instead of building clarity and commitment we had unwittingly contributed to a sense of powerlessness, frustration and inertia within the group. We began to see the possible role we had played in contributing to the persistence of the circular arguments and reinforcing the dysfunctional blockages that we saw enacted over and over again in individual conversations and workshops.

We also noticed, for the first time, that the project had focused almost exclusively on the internal workings of the university and the current practices of staff. This had proven unproductive because a fundamental purpose of the capability approach to curriculum was to better prepare students to act effectively in the external professional and civic worlds they would enter upon graduation. We thought that an external focus might help to break the inward, blaming, competitive 'us/them' dynamic with a more outward, collaborative, 'we're all in this together' one.

Turning to our conceptions of ourselves as learning leaders in this form of professional development, we needed to face some unpleasant possibilities. Perhaps our desire for the project to be 'owned' by the team members meant that we had hesitated to take the initiative and suggest directions or possibilities. As leaders we didn't want to 'tell them the answer', but we could take a more active role in summarizing and reflecting back to the group possible interpretations from their thinking. This would provide a focus for further reflection and action, and if done carefully we could move the team forward while avoiding the danger of speaking for the group.

We resolved to spend the next workshop reflecting with the group on where we were with the project, how we had got there, and we hoped to guide them to an agreement that for a short while they would suspend disbelief and engage in some constructive action. Two forms of action came to mind. We could tackle some more structured workshops to develop a profile of the kinds of capability a graduate from the Bachelor of Commerce should possess. Second, we would plan a conference for all the stakeholders for the degree – industry, students, alumni, university representatives from related project areas. This would provide an opportunity to deepen our understanding of the emerging professional environment and the nature of capable practice for a beginning business graduate.

We adopted some specific practices that we hoped would contribute to building a safer and more creative working environment. First, we would only distribute agendas for the workshops a couple of days in advance. Our aim was to reduce the opportunities for factional groupings to plan their positions before the group activity or discussion had taken place. We would also make sure that agendas were based on openly framed questions or activities that would encourage engagement with clearly defined aspects of the work. Establishing an electronic forum also seemed like a good idea. This would allow conversation between workshops, contribute to a sense of group identity, but most importantly allow comments to be made or alternative suggestions to be posted with a greater distance than is possible in face to face contexts. This might allow 'space' for initial angry or dismissive responses to be calmed or reconsidered before workshops, and contribute to more considered and careful interactions.

Armed with these ideas we approached the next workshop. On the way we confided to each other a sense of considerable trepidation. It all seemed so clear and reasonable when we talked with each other, but some of the clarity and confidence evaporated as we neared the room. It was with some relief but also consternation that we discovered Tony was not attending. In his absence the team took a more constructive approach, and even though many issues remained unaddressed, the team reached agreement on some immediate actions.

The team decided that our next event would be a type of role play. All the school representatives would imagine themselves as the heads of the relevant departments within a large company. In this role they would explain to a new graduate undertaking a rotation in each department what he or she was expected to do. From this we wanted to extract a profile of capabilities.

On the day of the role play workshop we arrived early to cover the walls with butchers' paper so we could capture the outcomes from the imagined conversations. All was in readiness and we waited for all the school representatives to arrive. We had just reviewed the purpose of the workshop and how we might make a start when Tony came in late. He sat quietly for a while but then, unable to contain himself any longer, intervened explosively. 'I can't work with butchers' paper. We should be using electronic tools to do this work. This is the height of hypocrisy. We can't do this work cold. No one is prepared. It's a waste of time.'

Shock made us calm. Robyn patiently explained the decisions of the previous workshop, and while it would be wrong to suggest that we had complete support or a high level of conviction from the team, there was sufficient support to give it a go and learn together. We asked him to reconsider, to stay and to contribute. He hesitated for a while but then packed his papers and left. The workshop concluded with a bundle of disorganized butchers' paper scrawls, but from this our first profile of capabilities began to take shape.

Something had to be done about Tony's persistent and aggressive behaviour. There were enough indicators that we were starting to form as a learning community that the team reluctantly decided we would approach Tony's head of school and request he be replaced with a new representative.

In the following workshops we collectively reviewed the capability profile, reshaped it and started to tackle more detailed issues about how capability might develop and what levels of capability development might mean. How would we handle complexity? Would we start with simple situations and make them more complex as the student progressed? Or might we start with all the complexity of real business situations and just expect different levels of performance from more junior students? As a group we were starting to tease out what the concept of a capability-based curriculum might mean for this degree, as well as for our personal practice.

In parallel we organized external consultants to design and facilitate the stakeholder conference. We chose external consultants because we felt it was important at this stage to bring an outsider's view to our work. Based on a search conference methodology, the facilitators asked participants to review trends in the external environment and identify the kinds of relationships, alliances and resources that would be needed to complete successfully the design and delivery of the Bachelor of Commerce degree.

The conference was well attended, with a good mix of employers, students, academics and managers from supporting functions across the university. Management from within the faculty was less well represented. The conference began well, with some very useful input concerning environmental trends. Employers and students reviewed the draft profile of capabilities and were very enthusiastic about the approach. Some suggestions regarding changes of emphasis or the extension of capabilities were made, and these could easily be incorporated. It seemed we were on a roll. It was when we started to consider the context for further development and delivery that this pleasant illusion was shattered.

All the old issues resurfaced along with some new ones. There was a great deal of uncertainty whether the degree was to be offered in an Australian context or at an off-shore location. There was also confusion about the mode of delivery. While we were designing for a mixed mode approach with a significant amount of face to face interaction, some participants had heard that the degree was to be fully online. And the old issue of money came up. A couple of participants expressed the view that it was 'a very fine and lovely educational idea' but there was no way the degree proposed could be offered at the off-shore location for the fees negotiated. In the absence of the faculty managers who could clarify these issues, the last session of the conference was a debacle. Participants tried to plan actions for the next stage, but there was little conviction that the effort would serve any useful purpose. It seemed we were again victims of continuing ambiguity and uncertainty, and in the final session participants expressed their frustration by turning aggressively on the conference facilitators.

Too tired and depressed to think productively, we shambled off to the pub for what felt like a wake. But we couldn't let it go. We asked ourselves over and over again, 'What is going on here?' How did this happen? Had the team become so caught up in the development of the capability profile and the design of the degree that we had lost touch with the direction that senior faculty decision makers wanted the programme to take? In overcoming many of the dysfunctional dynamics within the team we had managed to create a learning community, but clearly this was not enough. Again, it all seemed too hard, but at least we had a weekend to think about it.

What options do the project leaders have?
What would you do in this situation?
How could the project leaders have dealt more effectively with the tension between the task of designing the programme and managing the broader organizational context?

PART 3

It was the first e-mail we opened when we returned to work. Simply titled 'The Bachelor of Commerce', it contained a short video clip with the message from one of the design team members, 'This is what it feels like.' The video was of a small, green, one-eyed, animated creature on stage singing the Gloria Gaynor song *I Will Survive*. She walks tentatively toward the viewer but increasingly gains in confidence until she is belting out the tune with conviction. Just as she reaches the climax a mirror ball, previously out of frame, drops from above and squashes her completely. This, indeed, was how it felt. But what should we do?

The design team met for a review session. Because the team was now well formed, with a core group working very effectively on the programme design, the setback served to reinforce the sense of team identity. As we reflected on the workshop, the team felt that its work had become isolated from other groups within the faculty, in particular the managers who would make key decisions about such issues as mode and place of delivery.

From this point the project continued on two fronts. One involved the design team working long and hard to develop, detail and document the design for accreditation. The other involved us in attempting to create a learning environment that connected the work of the team with the faculty's managers.

The first of these worked effectively, with the design team practices drawing on the lessons learned in the earlier part of the development. We could rely on this group to keep working through the educational issues to invent ways of going from our now endorsed capability profile to a detailed programme design. We had successfully created a vibrant and collaborative learning community around this task.

As leaders we continued to take more responsibility for arriving at propositions for how we might take educational concepts and develop ways to use these for design. The balance of leadership changed, however, as other members were able to contribute their greater expertise regarding business practices, and current and possible approaches to teaching and learning. As a team we invented methods of mapping the capabilities over the curriculum, and ways to communicate the specific responsibilities of individual, concurrent and follow on courses to those who would develop them in detail.

The work was never easy intellectually but the team dynamics were much less fraught. Quite often, the substance of the work and the dynamics of doing the work would come together. We found ourselves saying, 'You know, we are designing a programme where students will develop a whole range of capabilities we don't have! If only we knew how to work in a team and to engage respectfully with professionals from different practice cultures!' But now it was possible to have vigorous discussions. It was much more likely that these would end with, 'Yes, yes, I see where you're coming from', 'We're on the same train', 'Let's do it', 'Let's try that.'

The work continued to be both hard and exciting. The accreditation document captured much of the learning from this process, and generated new ideas that have been incorporated into the university's programme approval and Quality Assurance processes. Senior managers in the university commended the design as an exemplar for the university, and congratulated the design team on the quality of its work.

The outcome of the search conference had clearly identified shortcomings of not involving faculty management in the project. The engagement of academic staff was critical, but without the ongoing commitment and support of faculty leadership it would be impossible to deal effectively with the impact of the complex, evolving and potentially competing educational and management priorities on the programme.

We had made presentations and sent reports to faculty managers early in the process, but we had failed to establish effective and ongoing dialogue. Clearly the leadership group were driven by different pressures and priorities, and seemed unable, or unwilling, to engage with the problematic issues that had emerged from the project.

The review report from the stakeholder conference was rejected, and a proposed forum between the faculty leadership and the facilitators of the stakeholder conference was cancelled at short notice. We had requested this forum to try to consider openly the contentious issues that had vexed the conference itself. Subsequent attempts at dialogue and requests for reconsideration of the project timeline and delivery mode resulted in increasingly hostile and truncated meetings. Finally we were advised that no further discussion would be entered into, and we should 'do what we were told'. This we did, but with grave misgivings about the likelihood that the innovations embedded within the programme design would be realized in practice.

As a final contribution Robyn conducted an evaluation of the project. All those who had been involved in the project were invited to participate in an unstructured interview to describe their experiences and reflect on what they had learnt. From members of the design team there was often a strong acknowledgement of learning. 'I learned so much from you two about what a capability curriculum means, how to do it.' This learning was clouded, however, by a sense of confusion and distress concerning why it had proved so difficult. A number of the managers declined to participate in the interviews. Those who did reflected upon their lack of connection, and the sense that this project had in many ways threatened their sense of control and ownership of their school's contribution, challenged their perception of their professionalism, and in these ways been disempowering.

Could different approaches have been taken to connect management into the project?
Have you experienced a similar situation when attempting action learning based professional development? If so, how did you handle it?

CASE REPORTERS' DISCUSSION

This case raises a number of issues for professional developers adopting an action learning approach to staff development. When addressing non-routine or novel problem situations the approach has much to recommend it, and it is for this reason that recently it has gained considerable support within staff development units. Its advantages stem from the fact that the kinds of educational problem tertiary academics are now being asked to face require the invention or discovery of new knowledge and practices, and not the simple application of well-codified knowledge for their solution.

In addition, academics find themselves working in an environment characterized by high levels of change and uncertainty. Australian universities have suffered from significant decreases in government funding per student, and have introduced many initiatives to address this, including extensive international recruitment. Concurrent managerial reforms have resulted in recurring restructures, declining staff morale and lowered confidence about continuing employment. As this case demonstrates, this environment makes an action learning approach necessary but at the same time makes undertaking it fraught with difficulty.

Successful use of an action learning approach in this context requires commitment to, understanding of, and a willingness to participate in the learning by staff within all these sections of the university. In this case, a successful action learning team was established at the immediate task level despite early difficulties. This team, however, was not complemented by connected action learning teams at the faculty management or university leadership levels. To create this cascade of action learning teams requires considerable rethinking of the roles of academic managers, which complement the necessary learning that academic staff undertake as they reshape their understandings of teaching and learning and the nature of academic work.

What about Tony? For these outcomes to be achieved some significant changes were made in the design team, of which the removal of Tony was simply the most dramatic. Another staff member recognized that he was ill equipped for the task and did not want to undertake the necessary learning. He replaced himself. In the final work there was a dynamic core who carried the learning, together with a few more peripheral participants. Given the complex institutional environment outlined above, can we expect more than this? Learning in this way represents a significant challenge for many academics. It is unreasonable to expect that all will learn at the same rates. This suggests that if action learning is to be adopted it needs to be endorsed as a continuing staff development mode. Over various iterations and with the evidence of persistence and success, more and more academics may develop confidence and be willing to take the risks that jumping into uncertainty requires.

Questions for personal reflection

- Do you think action learning approaches can be successfully used for staff development in tertiary settings?
- How would you go about creating the organizational conditions for action learning to be successful?
- Is it possible to build effective and sustainable action learning teams at an operational level without parallel development of action learning teams at management levels?

CHAPTER 11

BETTER TOGETHER

Case reporter: Anne Oxley

Issue raised

The issue raised in this case is how to encourage and support staff to engage with inter-professional teaching and learning.

Background

This case takes place at Sheffield Hallam University. A successful bid to HEFCE's Fund for the Development of Teaching and Learning (FDTL) supported the creation of an inter-professional curriculum and more collaborative working in the recently merged School of Environment and Development – including Planning, Architecture, Housing, Building and Surveying. The project, 'Better Together', aimed to stimulate the development of an inter-professional curriculum in the built environment. It had a national focus which enabled the school to benefit from expertise and experiences elsewhere. As well as Sheffield Hallam University, the project involved Oxford Brookes and Kingston universities.

The case reporter is the full-time project manager. Her team includes a part-time researcher and three other 0.2 fte academic staff, and there is a budget of £250,000 over three years.

PART 1

'But we are already cooperating with each other. We do put our students together for some lectures. What's the problem?'

This was the reaction of one colleague when I asked if he was interested in exploring a more inter-professional curriculum. I had heard this and similar comments many times in recent months. I also heard, 'I'm an architect not a planner', and 'You don't understand. Our students come here to be surveyors, not learn about architecture.' But most disturbing for me was the comment, 'My subject's curriculum is already completely full as we have to meet all the professional competencies as set down by our professional institute, so we can't possibly leave anything out, let alone include a surveying module.'

Why had we started on what sometimes felt like an impossible quest? We knew that our colleagues weren't being deliberately awkward – health professionals encouraged to move to inter-professional education had been saying similar things for many years. Our colleagues believed strongly in the professional importance of what they taught. They often found the concept of inter-professional education threatening. So, when faced with the challenge of yet more change, they were inclined to barricade themselves even further behind their own professional walls – exactly the opposite of what we were hoping to achieve!

So why had we started on the project? Why were we as a school trying to develop inter-professional education if we knew there were such high levels of resistance? Should we not have learnt from our previous merger experiences that this was never going to be an achievable objective? How were we ever going to answer that very big question on many colleagues' lips, 'But how do you know that inter-professional education is more beneficial than single discipline teaching?'

For us, the two big reasons centred on employability and quality. We were concerned about:

- falling enrolments in some subject areas;
- changing employment environment;
- government concern that different professional graduates who play a significant part in creating the built environment often just didn't work together very effectively;
- reports suggesting that higher levels of inter-professional working practice would result in better end products and more effective processes.

Why don't the various professions work better together? The systems and procedures may be wrong, with deep-seated historical divisions between the members of the various professions involved. And the government, as well as many employers, suspect members of the professions just don't have the skills, the knowledge and the attitudes required to work together. We had to keep reminding ourselves, 'There is no choice here. This has to be the way forward for our school to survive and to succeed.'

We started the project believing that everything necessary to advance inter-professional education was already in place. Well, nearly everything. We were receiving some warning signals from staff in other universities. 'This is nothing new; we've been looking at this for the past 20 years and we're still no further forward.' Now staff developers often hear this line from those they try to work with. Sometimes it is true; sometimes it clearly means, 'Go away and stop bothering us!' On further examination, we saw that both explanations were true!

Engagement with inter-professional education was, in different places, variously thriving, patchy, and non-existent. Why weren't some people engaging? We delved further with our colleagues in the department. The reasons for not engaging were plentiful: 'We'd love to, but it would be too costly', 'We've tried to before, but it never works because of how the school is structured', and that old stand-by, 'The professional bodies would never accredit it.'

We also had some staff saying they did deliver inter-professionally, but on closer inspection this turned out to be nothing more than joint modules. When we reflected this back to them (albeit gently), they had a tendency, understandably, to become very defensive.

We knew that this was not going to be plain sailing! But we still believed deep down that all we had to do in our own school was to share all our findings and experiences of inter-professional education; highlight what we felt to be the 'compulsory' elements; bring together the different disciplines to discuss the benefits and rewards of inter-professional education; and get people to work together by introducing them to the common areas of each other's disciplines. They would, as a result of our efforts, move towards changing attitudes and approaches to teaching and learning. That was the initial plan, such as it was!

'Determined, and guardedly optimistic.' If you'd asked us how we felt at this stage of the project we'd probably have said something like that – a reasonable mind-set at the start of a development project! We felt passionately about the strengths and benefits of what we were promoting. We also had well-informed project staff – and some project money. How could we find the right drivers to bring staff together to work and teach collaboratively?

What do you think of the initial strategy to promote inter-professional collaboration?
What other factors should the team be aware of at this stage of the project?
What would you have done next?

PART 2

We started by surveying built environment employers and alumni. They confirmed what the government was saying – effective inter-professional collaboration was vital, and education was a key way to deliver it. The employment environment was changing; new disciplines were emerging, heavily concerned with collaborative, inter-professional practice. We had representatives of five professional accrediting bodies from the built environment area on our project steering group, who took a variety of lines on inter-professional education. All were very keen verbally, but often less so on paper and in practice.

We reflected that what we were ultimately trying to change in our own school was nothing less than the whole approach to inter-professional education. This included changes in curriculum design and content, in ways of working and teaching, and ways of thinking about education. It included all the associated changes in ethos and attitude. We realized that the project alone could not achieve this. Our legacy would be the networks and mechanisms we were able to put into place. Our methods had to be incremental and generative.

One possible driver was strong persuasion, or even compulsion, nationally or institutionally. We had very mixed feelings about this. We knew that things not perceived as essential or required simply don't get done. But we feared the culture of compliance – 'I'll do it because I must, but don't expect me to put my heart into it' – which can accompany compulsion. We could already sense that this type of resistance was in the air. Come to think of it, why, when inter-professional education had been on the agenda for so many years, were we still wondering how to implement it in a way that would stick?

How can the project team take the development of inter-professional education forward?
How can inter-professional education be made appealing to lecturers?
Is compulsion a viable option?

PART 3

'That's the only way to move forward,' I said. 'A much more complex, multi-faceted approach.' The project team was reviewing its progress and actions to date at its regular monthly meeting, and feeling rather dispirited. We had already identified some key players in the school, but given the extent and complexity of the challenges, we needed to find more, and to bring them on board at the earliest possible stage.

We worked top-down, bottom-up and from a number of different sides. We had the clear support of the acting director of school to drive the agenda forward. We contacted colleagues in our own school who we knew delivered inter-professional modules. They gave us case studies in which they reflected on how they had overcome issues such as resistant colleagues, timetabling difficulties and large student groups. We used these case studies to talk to other staff, and gradually began to identify a group of interested academics whom we saw as potential 'champions'.

But what about compulsion? Along with the compulsion to move towards some appropriate form of inter-professional education, we also had to offer lots of freedom for the department and individuals to work out how they would implement it.

We did more on a practical front to embed the concept of inter-professional education in the school. I became a member of the school's multi-disciplinary Learning and Teaching Committee. We ran a series of lunchtime seminars to raise staff awareness. We wrote articles for the school newsletter. We circulated flyers to all academic staff about inter-professional collaboration. We ran work-shops at school 'away-days'. An inter-professional special interest group was set up in the school as a direct result of 'away-day' discussions.

As these strategies came into place, we again started to feel more confident, but this was a more sophisticated and much better-informed confi-dence than we had felt at the outset. Yet there were still many staff we had not reached. And there were those who just saw the entire thing as a 'project' with which they did not have to engage. 'How's the project going?' they would ask when we passed in the corridor. At least they knew it existed, but this wasn't enough.

Continuing to work top-down and bottom-up we set up, under the direction of our acting head of school, an internal mixed-discipline task team to address inter-professional learning and teaching within the school. The team included all the heads of undergraduate programmes, a representative of the postgraduate programmes, myself and the acting director. It was to act as a 'think tank' to look at inter-professional curriculum design and school structures, and to reach out to all the subject areas. The members of the team had the responsibility to cascade the proposals down and to engage their own subject teams.

Twelve months after the project had begun, the task team had its first meeting. I was shocked. The discussions were the same ones we as project members had engaged in a year earlier. The objections to inter-professional education were the same ones we had heard before we started the project. We members of the project team had come a long way in developing our own understanding of inter-professional education. For the most part we hadn't brought our colleagues with us. I realized, with a heavy heart, that we needed to go right back to basics.

After some deliberation, we agreed that bringing all the school's staff along, at different levels and at varying paces, was vital to the process. It was decided that the task team would feed back into the special interest group, with myself as the link member. The special interest group would develop the ideas raised by the task team at a more practical level. Thus more key staff would drive this agenda forward.

Yet we still spent a lot of time listening to lecturing staff telling us what would not work and why. We had already spoken with enough staff from other institutions who had embraced inter-professional education (albeit with varying levels of success and resistance from staff) to have some answers with which to challenge what lecturers were telling us. We included some of the barriers and solutions we heard about from other institutions in a guidance manual we wrote on inter-professional education, being aware of course that anything had to be translated into our own institutional context if staff were to engage with it.

So have we overcome the challenges we identified earlier? Well – partly. Interested staff from different disciplines have volunteered to become members of the special interest group. Realizing the need for specific 'hooks', we have explored with other staff how the introduction of an inter-professional curriculum would fit into both the school's business plan and its learning and teaching strategy. We have set aside more time to work with staff at the next school 'away-day'. We have identified some specific areas of the curriculum where greater collaboration could take place.

We have also set out some plans for the future – both for the school and for the project as a whole. A paper proposing the school's comprehensive commitment to inter-professional education has recently been approved by the Board of Studies – a real achievement, we felt, that built on a lot of groundwork by the project team. We also have lots of plans for future activities to ensure the journey to inter-professionality is a rewarding one for both staff and students.

What do you think of the overall approach that was taken?
Is staff development for inter-professional education necessarily different from staff development for other purposes?
What would you have done differently?
What lessons could be learnt in your own subject area and at your own institution?

CASE REPORTER'S DISCUSSION

As I reflect on the approaches we have taken to engaging academic staff in inter-professional education, three questions come to mind:

- Would a more single-minded, intensive, focused approach, perhaps with just a few staff, have been more effective?
- Is it ever possible to overcome all the barriers to the introduction of inter-professional education?
- And finally, what more could we still do?

I come back to a multi-faceted approach as the only way this type of staff engagement could have taken place. Perhaps the main learning for us was that a balanced mix of top-down, bottom-up and sideways-in approaches was crucial. We learnt who it was vital to engage with – in this instance, primarily the school's executive team, one of the pro vice chancellors (who in this case also happened to be acting head of the school), the relevant subject leaders, both the undergraduate and postgraduate programme leaders, Learning and Teaching Committee members and Learning and Teaching Institute staff.

In engaging with staff to work inter-professionally, we are not just bringing together a group of staff to work on what they are going to do about lecturing methods, for example, or writing unit descriptors. We sometimes feel that we are challenging their professional status, the attitudes and ethos they each bring with them from their particular discipline, the traditional ways in which they have worked, at least as teachers, and perhaps also as practitioners of their discipline.

But surely some of them had successful experiences of inter-professional working before they became lecturers? We may not have sufficiently drawn on these experiences in the project so far. This deserves further consideration. Inter-professional education requires people to:

- work together across different disciplines/professions;
- adopt a mind-set and ethos that includes open-mindedness, creativity, a willingness to negotiate and collaborate;
- alter their working practices;
- re-evaluate their approaches to teaching and learning;
- some degree at least get inside disciplines other than their own, and develop some understanding of how these other disciplines think and work.

Each of these alone requires a massive effort.

We came to recognize that many of the perceived barriers to engaging staff in inter-professional education can be moved aside. Talking to staff, sharing experiences, putting people in touch with other institutions and making suggestions for distinct new approaches all contributed significantly to this movement.

We acknowledged from the start the importance of the enthusiasm and sustained commitment of interested staff. We saw how they were able to drive forward inter-professional education. We also saw how their enthusiasm often rubbed off on other staff, particularly when they received positive feedback from students and from external examiners on the new educational approaches they were adopting. Likewise, the collaboration between the project staff and the school academic staff, with the latter acting as key personnel from within to effect change, was very important.

We are still in the first phase of what will no doubt be a prolonged process of staff engagement and development. Our approach to the introduction of inter-professional education has been to reach different staff in varying settings and with various concerns by using a range of methods. Strong support from above and a clear indication of the potential benefits have been important factors in what success we have achieved. We have also understood much better some of the many factors that help and hinder change.

The case study does not tell me how far the particular factors and issues and methods we encountered and used will apply in the development of inter-professional education across other subjects, and in staff and educational development more generally. Over to you, hopefully helped and selectively encouraged by our experiences.

CHAPTER 12

THE SEVEN STEPS

Case reporter: Jamie Thompson

Issue raised

The issue raised in this case is how a university can make academics feel more valued in their teaching role.

Background

Each UK university is required by the relevant funding council to produce a learning, teaching and assessment strategy. As part of this, the University of Northumbria established a 'Recognizing and Rewarding Teaching' Task Group. The task group consisted of learning, teaching and assessment coordinators from each faculty and members of the University Quality Enhancement Unit. The Task Force had a loose brief, 'to recommend criteria for recognizing and rewarding teaching, paying due attention to the HR implications and the representation of the student voice', and a small budget.

PART 1

Our first question to each other at the initial meeting of the 'Recognizing and Rewarding Teaching' Task Group was, 'What do you think the university expects us to produce?'

You'll see from this that we were tempted to see the task as essentially a pragmatic one, requiring us to devise some criteria for appointment to promoted teaching posts. We started down this road by looking in some detail at existing schemes elsewhere to introduce temporary and permanent teaching 'readerships' and 'professorships' and the like. We found that essentially these schemes take the traditional academic model of reward and recognition for excellence in research and scholarship, and apply it to excellence in teaching.

Soon, and I think rather to our surprise, we found ourselves deep in debate about the limitations of such schemes. We well understood the currency of these rewards. But we wondered whether such a scheme, certainly on its own, could substantially develop a 'teaching culture', or make most staff feel better about their teaching role. We kept on asking, 'Why are we doing this?' and 'What is this really all about?'

How is teaching recognized and rewarded in your institution?
What ways of recognizing and rewarding teaching could the team come up with?

PART 2

One important idea came out very strongly from our debate. We all believed that most staff who are engaged in helping students to learn want to do this job well. This immediately meant that recognizing and rewarding teaching was part of a much larger process. It was also necessary to identify and remove the barriers and constraints that prevented staff from reaching their full potential as teachers.

What to do with this? We felt we needed to explore the views and experiences of staff. We needed to ask them such questions as, 'Do you feel your teaching role is adequately recognized and rewarded?', 'What (if anything) stops you doing the teaching part of your job to your full potential?' and 'What (if anything) constrains the development of your professional excellence in teaching?'

To do this we explained the work of the task group to some teaching colleagues. We told them what we were trying to do. We asked for volunteers to tell us about (or indeed to show us) their teaching, and to identify the problems and difficulties they faced.

Volunteers came forward from across the university. We ran semi-structured, anonymous interviews. We asked them to tell us about their experience of teaching at the university. How much of their job, directly and indirectly, involved teaching? What was good about their teaching? What were they less happy about? What got in the way of improved teaching? Did they feel that their teaching was recognized and rewarded appropriately? What would need to happen for them to feel their teaching was better recognized and rewarded?

Interesting themes emerged from these interviews. There was good support for the notion of raising the profile of and rewarding teaching, but there was cynicism about whether there would actually be any change. Some described their concern that, far from increasing the value given to teaching, managers were pressing academic staff to reduce the overall volume of teaching. They felt that reducing the amount of time available for staff/student contact was inevitably reducing the quality of teaching. Staff levels were static and student numbers rising. In addition, some staff felt under increasing pressure to generate research and other income. They told us of a culture in which administration and research took people away from teaching. This provoked staff who saw themselves primarily as teachers to anger, frustration and anxiety.

Another significant theme was inequity. First, there was a clear sense that teaching was not related to any career development. We were told, 'In terms of promotion, teaching is a "Cinderella" activity compared with administration and research.' Increasingly, teaching was not informing administration and management, and research was not informing teaching. One research-active respondent told us of his frustration: 'I find it harder and harder to sustain my identity as a professional teacher *and* a researcher.' Many active researchers, he felt, were not making significant contributions to teaching; indeed, their research was largely unconnected even to courses and programmes to which it could clearly be relevant.

Our interviews elicited general support for teaching reward systems involving promotion routes, fellowships and small grant payments. But, alongside this, there was cynicism – 'All these fellowships and grants will do is take good teachers away from teaching.'

Finally and most consistently, staff identified what we might call hygiene factors – administrative load, teaching facilities and conditions – as central to their concerns:

- So-called quality systems waste time I should be spending on teaching.
- Every year there's more admin to do, and less support for doing it.
- I can't tell who's in charge of what any more.
- The first few weeks of term can be really rough, with timetabling and room problems.

Our hunch had been right. There was more to 'recognizing and rewarding teaching' than promotions. Barriers and constraints were indeed preventing staff from reaching their full potential as teachers.

We didn't abandon rewards. As well as running and analysing these interviews, we piloted Applauding and Promoting Teaching (APT). This was funded through the Higher Education Funding Council for England (HEFCE) initiative 'Rewarding and Developing Staff in HE'. Any member of staff contributing to student learning could apply, individually or on behalf of a team, for an award of £1–2,000 to support teaching development. Award winners committed themselves to disseminating their work at a University Teaching and Learning conference. The application process was kept as simple as possible, and the range of ways the monies could be used were as wide as possible. There was a substantial response from across all faculties, and over 30 awards were made totalling over £50,000.

It was time to reach some conclusions. We asked ourselves to what extent, and how, the task group should accommodate the findings of the research and the strong response to the APT scheme. We put together a comprehensive and ambitious package of proposals on recognizing and rewarding teaching. We disseminated them very widely, and asked for responses from all relevant staff. We received lots of responses, written and through debate at consultation meetings. Finally we put together seven proposals:

1. **Attention is needed to hygiene factors.** This first proposal expressed our belief that in fact staff want to be able to teach to the best of their ability. The wholehearted adoption and active implementation of steps to address hygiene factors would be seen as a strong message to staff and students that teaching was valued. Classroom environments, equipment and support services should be fit for purpose. Administrative and academic rules and procedures should not constrain a flexible and effective approach to teaching and learning.

2. **Membership of the Institute for Learning and Teaching in Higher Education should be paid for all eligible members of staff.** This proposal was to continue an existing pilot scheme.

3. **Continuing Professional Development (CPD).** Many training and development opportunities were offered across the university, but there was still no framework and process of staff development that could be used strategically and as a platform for scholarly and professional debate about teaching and learning in the modern university. We proposed building a strategic, comprehensive and coherent framework for continuing professional development including opportunity for accreditation.

4. **Learning teaching and assessment coordinator posts should be continued.** These were half-time posts, one in each faculty, initially funded for two years. The consultation had suggested that they were valued, and should be continued. A small study of staff views of the University Learning Teaching and Assessment policy said the same. We saw the role of learning teaching and assessment coordinator as a vital link between central policy and local best practice. Top-down, the coordinators could promote a more consistent understanding of university priorities and policy. Bottom-up, they could make sure that policy development was informed by what was happening across the institution. And they could continue to act as catalysts and disseminators of best practice.

5. **An annual 'recognition of teaching' award.** We proposed to continue the Applauding and Promoting Teaching (APT) awards

already described. The emphasis here was on simple and transparent criteria. Applicants would be asked simply to describe the context of their teaching, the work they were engaged with or wanted to start, what outcomes were anticipated, and how the work related to the development of teaching and learning at the university and to their own professional development. We also suggested that the award should offer a menu of possible benefits that reflect the different needs of staff at different stages of their career. For some, the funding might support training and development activity; for others, it would be used to meet particular costs, 'buy time' for project staff activity or even fund cash payments for award winners, perhaps as overtime payments.

6. **An annual 'dissemination of pedagogical practice' award.** This would give timetable remission of up to 200 hours over two years. The staff involved would have to spend that time working with colleagues to develop their teaching, or team-teaching with them.

7. **A promotion route and career path for effective teachers.** We wanted a way to keep effective teaching staff, not only within the university, but also still in direct contact with students. We did not want to diminish current promotion criteria based on excellence in research and management. We did want to give teaching excellence equivalence with management and research. New 'lead teacher' posts were proposed at principal lecturer/readership level.

This package, however good, still had to be approved by the major decision-making bodies, the Learning Teaching and Assessment Committee, and assuming their approval the University Executive Committee. How would our proposals fare in the cut and thrust of university decision making?

What do you think of the proposals that were made?
What other proposals would you have suggested?
How do you think the approval committees will react to the proposals?

PART 3

We need not have worried. Both the Learning Teaching and Assessment Committee and the University Executive Committee approved the proposals for Recognizing and Rewarding Teaching, and they were included in university plans for the forthcoming year. But implementing the seven proposals inevitably presented challenges.

With 'Attention is needed to hygiene factors' we face difficulties in setting targets and then measuring improvement. The continuing improvement of classroom resources and support requires funding, and management will. Appropriate lines of accountability and responsibility for this are in place, but administrative and academic rules and processes seem a much more difficult problem to overcome. We may adopt a rational economic approach, with cost–benefit analyses of various possible classroom improvements, followed, of course, by evaluation. What kinds of benefits might we expect? We might achieve university and government priorities such as widening participation in higher education; improving student retention; education for employability; and better accommodating students with additional needs. We know this work will be difficult, but we need sound arguments and data to make the case for resources.

'Membership of the Institute for Learning and Teaching in Higher Education paid for all eligible members of staff': the question now is how to evaluate the impact and benefits of the scheme and more broadly the benefits of ILTHE membership. In the long term, impact on teaching quality may be the best indicator.

'Continuing Professional Development (CPD)': work on the CPD proposal has begun with the human resources department. It raises a range of interesting questions. How voluntary should participation be? How will it fit with the current compulsory programme for new teachers? How will the framework relate to current appraisal processes?

'Learning teaching and assessment coordinator posts': these posts have now been continued for a further year, when they will be reviewed again. Again, questions remain. Should the posts continue to be half-time? Drawing on their own current teaching practice gives the coordinators animation and credibility, but the demands of the job are substantial. How should the coordinators be managed? To what extent should they be owned locally?

'Annual "recognition of teaching" award': the APT scheme had proved successful. It had attracted large numbers of bidders keen to work on a wide range of teaching issues, and a university conference on Teaching and Learning was built around papers and presentations from award winners, and was also very successful. The unresolved issue here is whether or not it will prove possible to offer (taxable) cash payments to award winners. This proved impossible to negotiate for the pilot APT scheme, where the award had to be spent on buying out teaching time, in funding project costs or in funding staff development activity.

'Annual "dissemination of pedagogical practice" award': this role might make a considerable impact, but how many such award holders are an optimum number? And how would their work be evaluated?

'Promotion route and career path for effective teachers': details of this are currently being discussed with the human resources department.

CASE REPORTER'S DISCUSSION

We tried to take a much broader and more strategic approach to recognizing and rewarding teaching, at the same time including standard expectations such as awards and promotions. Shaw *et al* (1978) describe a model for understanding competence (and confidence) in a work role. The model says that role competence (and I would add role confidence) is only possible when three factors come together:

- **adequacy:** the knowledge and skills required for the job;
- **legitimacy:** a clear understanding about the expectations of the role, legal, professional, organizational (What am I expected to do?);
- **support:** material, managerial, emotional, professional and supervisory support as required.

How did we relate this model to our goal to boost the recognition and rewarding of teaching?

Adequacy

What knowledge and skills are needed to teach in higher education? This is a complex area. Clearly teachers need high levels of subject knowledge. Some theoretical understanding of how learning takes place is also important. Teaching requires a wide range of skills, from specific written and verbal communication skills to awareness of and ability to use different technologies. And all of these require continual maintenance and development.

Universities work hard to recruit academic staff with sufficient subject knowledge, and they have established criteria for judging this – academic qualifications, research experience and publication. Assessing the adequacy of knowledge and skills for teaching is less easy. Our university has bitten the bullet with a compulsory programme for new lecturers.

A bigger question than the adequacy of new staff is that of existing staff. Again, we assume in higher education that teaching staff maintain high levels of expertise and knowledge in their subject areas. Most quality assurance systems check that at least the content of taught programmes is current and at an appropriate level. Quality assurance systems allow for scrutiny of proposed teaching and learning approaches, but in themselves don't offer a process for development and improvement of practice. Peer observation and feedback are becoming more widespread, and offer a start. But these depend on staff willingness to engage in critical debate. Are there relevant training opportunities available at the right time? Do staff have time to engage in them? Adequacy isn't just about the individual – it is about the individual in their particular work context.

Our proposal for a strategic CPD framework begins to address these issues. Challenges remain. Will the framework be flexible enough to meet needs as they arise? How will it be linked to individual and institutional needs? Will engagement with CPD be compulsory, for some (who?) or all?

How will CPD link to appraisal processes? Whatever the answers, time to develop and maintain appropriate levels of adequacy must be protected.

Legitimacy

Do employers have a clear and unambiguous sense of what they expect from academic teaching staff? Some academic staff are recruited to engage in research only, with the expectation that they will generate income both directly and indirectly for the university. Elsewhere we hear that other staff are recruited on teaching-only contracts, and paid on lower scales. Meanwhile, for most academic staff, there is an assumption that their role involves teaching, scholarly activity and also administration. But how does an individual know the priority?

Answering this, and the many similarly difficult questions, needs dialogue between the institution and the individual member of staff. The result of the dialogue should be that members of staff have a clear sense of the parameters within which they are working, and an agreed development plan for their future. The result for the university should be a clear sense of how each member of staff will contribute to the work of the organization, and of what resources will be necessary to support and develop this contribution.

Academics, like other professionals, need a strong personal sense of legitimacy. They must also understand their legitimacy in terms of what the institution expects and needs. This cannot happen unless middle and senior managers in universities are also confident about their own legitimacy, and establish and lead strong staff appraisal and development processes which will accommodate the purpose, aims and objectives of the university and the potential, skills and aspirations of each member of staff.

Support

Teachers in higher education need support to do their jobs. Some of this support is implicit in the discussion earlier about adequacy and legitimacy. To spell it out, lecturers need education and training opportunities, a robust CPD framework, and unambiguous dialogue through appraisal processes. These will all support the development of confidence and competence. Similarly, engagement with peers around teaching and learning issues, through peer observation and review, and teaching team meetings, further supports a professional approach.

Most academic roles include various levels of administration and management. The skills, knowledge, experience and time to undertake the work associated with this need to be secured. There may well be important training and development needs, perhaps particularly for those taking on management roles. More broadly, administrative arrangements need continuing review. Do administrative arrangements support teaching staff? Are administrative processes developed with reference to the role of teaching staff? Is there enough administrative support? Could the institution release academic time for teaching through more administrative support? Which tasks are routine and which are more complex and managerial? And are lines of accountability and authority always clear?

The support systems needed for teaching are becoming ever more sophisticated and technological. These in turn bring training and development needs. Alongside growth in skills and knowledge, the university must also respond to the practical needs of teachers. Do the available rooms and equipment meet the demands of the teaching work? Are rooms the right size? Are rooms appropriately equipped? Are timetabling processes sufficiently sensitive to particular needs? Are rooms and technology reliable and well maintained? Is help quickly available in the event of problems? Is the rooming and equipment available to individual academic staff fit for purpose? Are there appropriate spaces for academic staff to meet together both formally and informally?

The initial brief of the project was 'to recommend criteria for recognizing and rewarding teaching, paying due attention to the HR implications and the representation of the student voice'. Addressing this drew us to some fundamental and structural issues in the university, many of which were beyond the remit of the project. Our growing awareness of these issues as we undertook the project led us to conclusions and recommendations broader than we expected at the start. We think that our 'seven steps' have gone some way to recognizing the inter-relationship of staff development with other policy, structure and infrastructual arrangements of the university.

Reference

Shaw, S *et al* (1978) *Responding to Drinking Problems*, Croom Helm, London

CHAPTER 13

MISSION IMPOSSIBLE?

Case reporter: Veronique Johnston

Issue raised

The issue raised in this case is stimulating changes to culture and practice in order to enhance the student experience and improve students' chances of academic success.

Background

Napier is a mainly vocational university that has largely succeeded in its aim to recruit students from previously underrepresented groups. In 1994, the university realized that it knew and understood too little about how students were doing after they enrolled, about the links between student retention and the financial and reputational health of the institution, and about the activities required to keep students on course and succeeding in their studies.

The case reporter was a member of the university's Mathematics department who became leader of a Student Retention Project.

PART 1

Some projects start with a bang, with a shock. The Student Retention Project didn't. It started with a grumbling appendix, not a broken leg. It started with a nagging feeling that too many students were leaving the university before graduation, indeed in their first year with us; and with the feeling that the recent shift to a modular programme may have made this worse.

What do academics and administrators do with a feeling like this? They check out the facts. Michael, a senior university manager, agreed with Anne, director of quality, to find someone to look into it. But it turned out to be much more difficult to check out the facts than expected. 'Masses of data but very little information' fairly describes the situation.

Then we got lucky. The university had a new professor of statistics, and Gillian relished the chance to get stuck into a real statistical problem that would also help her get to know her new university better.

'It's worse than we thought.' Gillian had already warned us that her data on student retention would be depressing. One reason for this was technical – we had moved the date from which students were counted as being enrolled with the university. Previously we had only counted as 'enrolled' those students who were still with us on 31 January. 'Making this your baseline means that you miss all those students who drop out in the first three months,' Gillian pointed out. Her data took a much earlier starting point, but even allowing for that, we were still surprised and disappointed by the data. So was Michael, when we showed him the data at the meeting that Wednesday morning. We discussed our concerns.

'It's simply unethical to lose all these students from the university,' said Anne. 'Accepting a student onto a programme of study surely means accepting that the student has some reasonable prospect of success.' Gillian, Michael and I developed the argument. This reasonable prospect of success, of course, couldn't be unconditional. It required a reasonable and appropriate kind of effort on the part of both the student and university. But focusing on recruitment without regard for retention seemed to us all to be wrong, not least because of the potentially serious impact on real people's lives. Also, Napier was committed to providing students from a range of backgrounds and experiences with opportunities to succeed in higher education.

'And don't forget it's costing the university a lot of money,' said Michael. 'Students bring with them funds in each year of their studies. Students who do not complete their studies bring with them less income than if they complete.' We explored the economic side further. It was cheaper to hold a current student than attract a new one. Successful current customers who completed their course might return for further courses, buy consulting and research services, and recommend the university to friends, family, colleagues and employer. 'And don't forget that if we gain a reputation as a place that doesn't support our students, people will be less likely to apply in the future,' I added.

The fourth issue, we all agreed, was the quality agenda. The university had to understand, and if necessary improve, its performance before it was tested by external peers. Gillian's data, and the results of previous departmental reviews, suggested large differences in retention rates among programmes and departments. Why these variations?

Towards the end of the meeting, the inevitable question – what do we do now? With Michael's strong encouragement and funding, Anne and I set up what we decided in an upbeat and forward-looking moment to call the Student Retention Project (SRP). It was planned to run for one year. The total staffing consisted of part of me with smaller parts of Anne and Gillian and consistent high-level support from Michael. We set up an advisory group comprising representatives from the faculties and Napier's Students' Association. The idea was to continue to calculate programme pass rates, conduct a staff and student survey, find out what affected progression, and come up with some practical solutions.

We decided early in the life of the project to restrict the analyses to first-year undergraduates. Why? Because we already knew that first-year students suffered the highest drop-out rates and represented the largest single body undertaking one mode of study. (It is difficult to calculate progression rates for non-homogeneous programmes and modes of study.)

We soon found that we could identify just four non-overlapping categories of student outcomes – withdraw; fail; proceed carrying some modules to be completed later; and pass outright. Each of the four categories told us something different about the student experience. Withdrawal rates let us monitor recruitment, induction and the early student experience. Failure rates told us something about the academic experience and about how far students can recover from early failure. Failure rate also identified subject areas that students find more academically challenging. Rates of students proceeding carrying some modules to be completed later identified groups of students who might require additional academic support. Outright pass rates, of course, told us what proportion of students were coping successfully, and how that differed between subject areas. We were beginning to see the value of measuring student retention.

We also became aware of the complexity of the task. Data from the student record database needed considerable cleaning and manipulation to provide useful, easy-to-understand statistics. This took time and effort. Gillian oversaw this part of our research work to ensure high-quality data and academic credibility for the project.

We were still shocked by the low first-year pass rates that our research uncovered – they were even worse than the previous year's statistics. We were also worried, and not just by the wider concerns that Michael had offered. How would management and academics react to these results? We understood the sensitivities. We only showed to each head of department his or her own department's statistics, and we delivered the data in sealed envelopes marked 'confidential'.

How, we wondered, was Napier doing compared with other universities? Were our pass rates unusually low, was this an unusually bad year, or did our rates reflect a sectoral norm? In 1994, comparative data from other institutions were almost non-existent.

We found no studies from UK universities on strategies to improve retention. A main conclusion from North American research was the importance of context when developing retention strategies – and our context was very different from theirs! When Napier decided to learn how to improve retention rates, and to understand why some students do not succeed, we were on our own. We collected reliable and clean data on student pass rates for two years. We persuaded our academic colleagues that the data were correct. We had resources for a further year and we wanted to improve student retention. What could we do?

What options do the team have to improve retention rates?
How can they keep colleagues engaged, and retention on the university agenda?
Are retention rates a problem for your university? How do you tackle the issue?

PART 2

That first publication of first-year student pass rates raised more questions than it answered:

- How representative were the data?
- What factors influenced student retention?
- How well matched were staff perceptions of the reasons for student withdrawal and failure to the reality?

The first question could only be answered by a long-term commitment to producing year on year comparative retention statistics. With Anne and Michael's support, the commitment was made – student retention was, and still is, seen by the university as a fundamental quality issue. We decided to track first-year student pass rates by faculty, school, programme and a range of student groups for up to eight years, and second to fourth years for three years. We also added student return rates by previous outcome (that is, we calculated the return rates of students into one year by their academic outcome in the previous year), progress rates (the proportion of students who both passed and returned), and award rates.

The second question on factors influencing student retention led to a university-wide survey of first-year student backgrounds and motivations. This data was linked to individual student records. This comparison of survey responses with retention data enabled us to find out what had the greatest influence on student outcomes.

In a parallel strand of work we tackled the third question by comparing academic staff perceptions of the reasons students did not progress with the data they themselves held on students on their programmes. And we fed the results back to the staff.

Over time, we added to this list of enquiries. We have now also surveyed non-returners, withdrawn students and students who failed at the first assessment, among others. We also used surveys and interviews to compare what staff and students consider to be good teaching, again feeding the results back to the staff so that they could work out the implications for their own teaching.

However, we realized that research and publication were not enough. We decided early on that any SRP research must result in some practical outcome for either staff or students, so that they could appreciate the benefits of the work as well as the pain. We went about this by running many staff development events; publishing a good practice guide for staff; publishing a guide to developing teaching, learning and assessment strategies for new courses; supporting staff undertaking their own retention work; publishing for students a booklet 'What am I doing here anyway?' which aims to answer the 10 most important questions posed by students; publishing a Student Diary to promote time-management skills; and developing and supporting the use of a diagnostic test to identify students most at risk of withdrawal or failure.

During the life of the project, Napier has realized measurable improvements in student performance – for example, the proportion of first-year students passing all their modules has risen by 15 per cent since 1995/96. Student retention is widely accepted as a valid issue for discussion and action at all levels. All published reports are now available to every member of staff. Statistical reports on student performance are an established feature of university monitoring and review processes.

But we didn't get from there to here by following a master plan. There wasn't one. What we did was to try a range of strategies. In nine years we made our fair share of mistakes, which led us to change our approach, though not our goal. One thing we realized early on. It was not the 'Why?' or the 'What?' that provided the greatest challenge. They were clear enough. It was the 'How?' How do you change the focus on retention from rhetoric to action? How do you engage academics in the process? How do you know if anything is making a difference? We had a number of strategies.

We kept retention visible. In the early stages of retention work, once we had reliable data, we worked hard to raise the retention agenda with staff. Student non-completion is not a comfortable topic for many academics. As one head of department put it, 'These [student non-completion] data show us as much about our own failures as they do about student failures.' After a couple of years of the SRP you just couldn't be an academic at Napier without having to face the retention agenda.

We set priorities, targets and limits. Long-term achievable and fair pass rate targets have been set for each of the four years of our undergraduate degrees, and success is applauded. We are now within 1 per cent of achieving our overall first-year pass rate target, and are 9 per cent above our lowest point.

We worked hard to balance challenging established norms and **development of an open culture**, where retention could be discussed honestly without the fear of blame. This continues to challenge us. Some subject areas will probably always have poorer retention than others, so it is better to focus on achieving continuous improvement than on achieving parity. A positive and supportive attitude by management is essential, as is the open publication of retention statistics and the integration of a retention perspective into course design, approval, delivery and review.

Internalizing retention: increasingly, academic staff are encouraged to develop a self-reflective style during the review and evaluation of modules, programmes and schools, concentrating on how performance compares with previous years, what the main successes and challenges were, and what evidence they have to support their views.

We accepted that this was a long-term undertaking. But like many optimists, we underestimated just how long term. The cycle of research, action and evaluation takes a minimum of three years, and more likely four to five years. The university realized this. The Student Retention Project is now fully embedded into the Quality Enhancement Services budget. How did we achieve this? First, the director of Quality Enhancement Services strongly championed the project. Second, we delivered results – our emphasis on turning research into action was pivotal here. Third, the SRP provided external agencies with hard evidence of Napier's commitment to improving the student experience and to supporting student success. Lastly, as our work has continued, we have increasingly come to understand that the key to improving retention lies in achieving fundamental changes to the institutional culture – and that is very long-term work indeed.

We accepted that there was no single solution. A number of initiatives were led from the centre, but many initiatives were carried out within the faculties and schools. We encouraged a great variety of initiatives including staff development, paper guides, surveys and newsletters. In the early years our emphasis was on student support initiatives. We accepted that not all would succeed, and review points were built into all initiatives.

We gave great emphasis to **monitoring and evaluation**, so that we and the colleagues directly undertaking the work would know what was working, and how well, and why. Our least successful initiative was the publication of a good practice guide for staff. Although it was treated with interest, it didn't lead to a single example of changed practice!

We adopted a carrot and stick approach for staff. A project such as the SRP can only be an agent for change. Vital for improving retention are the enthusiasm and willingness of staff to embrace change. Publication of data was essential – but the publication of retention statistics can be felt as an attempt to embarrass or blame staff. To balance this we provided lots of practical support to staff, including workshops and one-to-one consultancy.

We encouraged the review of learning, teaching and assessment strategies. Learning, teaching and assessment issues were seen as crucial to improving retention, particularly as widening access has changed the skills, knowledge, goals and approaches that students at Napier bring to their studies. A cross-institutional project was set up to embed employability skills into the curriculum, and our Educational Development Service led the development and implementation of an over-arching learning, teaching and assessment strategy (LTAS) with retention at its core.

We assured the academic credibility of the work. The steering group contained a number of highly regarded academics who strongly contributed to the research element of our work. Second, the research assistant on the project was also a lecturer. A real understanding of and sympathy with the nature and rhythm of academic life was essential, and helped overcome much of the distrust that centrally led initiatives can engender.

How would these approaches and methods be received in your institution?

CASE REPORTER'S DISCUSSION

All retention projects start with good intentions, and often a great deal of zeal. They tend to be led by highly motivated individuals with a passion for improving the student experience. But effort alone does not guarantee success. Review is essential to ensure that zeal and passion are being directed in appropriate directions, and to acknowledge successes while learning lessons.

To review the breadth and balance of retention initiatives and to identify gaps in overall strategy, we adapted a model developed by Beatty-Guenter (1994) to review retention literature from community colleges in Canada. She identified five main categories of retention strategy – sorting, supporting, connecting, transforming the institution and transforming the student:

- **Sorting strategies** group students into appropriate subsets. They include pre-entry and threshold, the admissions process, assessment on entry, mechanisms to monitor student attendance and progress, and profiling 'at risk' students.
- **Supporting strategies** aimed to support students in their lives outside the university so that they find it easier to continue as students. They include financial help, child care provision, health promotion, transport provision and personal safety programmes.
- **Connecting strategies** develop and foster relationships between students and the institution, and help students integrate into college life by joining a community. Typical strategies include personal tutors, course events, peer support, faculty advisers and attendance monitoring.

- **Transforming the institution strategies** aim to improve all aspects of teaching and learning and the working environment – curriculum redesign, policy changes, action research programmes, cultural change, staff development programmes, teaching and learning innovations and so on.
- **Transforming the student strategies** attempt to transform the student in some way – for example from passive to active learners, from possessing poor skills to developing improved skills, or from expecting failure to expecting success. Such strategies include learning assistance, study skills development, academic counselling and careers counselling.

Beatty-Guenter concludes that any comprehensive retention programme, regardless of how small or large the programme is, must include some strategies from each category in order to be truly effective. This perspective definitely struck a chord with us. Our project had been running for about five years – how could we keep up the momentum? Were we really bringing about fundamental cultural change? Were we using our resources to their best effect? How could we best plan the next phase of our work?

We used the Beatty-Guenter typology to assess our achievements, review the scope and nature of our efforts and identify gaps in our strategy. An informal audit of our retention initiatives showed us that:

- There was considerably more sorting, supporting and connecting activity than transforming. Transforming strategies were small-scale and run by committed enthusiasts, with few mechanisms for rolling out good practice. The exception to this was 'Toolkit' which aimed to integrate study skills into all first-year undergraduate curricula.
- We saw a staged approach. We had initially concentrated more effort on sorting and supporting, followed by connecting strategies. Further analysis revealed that this was linked to a hierarchy of difficulty, effort and cost.
- Transformation initiatives only rarely had improved student retention as an explicit aim. They were much more likely to refer to aims such as improved student learning and better student experience, so their role in terms of retention was not always clearly acknowledged.

Other universities working to improve retention describe a pattern of activity – first addressing recruitment and admissions (sorting), then reorganizing student services (supporting), followed by improvements to induction and personal tutor processes (connecting). Transforming is rarer.

This pattern is understandable. Sorting and supporting initiatives tend to be small in scope. Such initiatives can assume that the students themselves are the retention problem – 'The student is not standard.' A major change in culture is needed to shift away from this view. Sorting and supporting work is valuable, but it isn't the whole story.

Connecting strategies acknowledge the interaction between students and the institution. Connecting strategies require institutions to make much more fundamental changes to processes and attitudes. But they often still only affect the working practice of a subset of staff (personal tutors, induction teams, faculty advisers and so on) or a relatively small part of the working practice of a broader group of staff (as with induction procedures).

Transformational strategies provide the greatest challenge for any institution because of the degree of cultural change that is necessary. Yorke (1999) notes that 'the problem with proposals to improve teaching has two dimensions. The first is the competition for attention that exists between teaching and research, in which the latter retains a commanding lead that is bolstered by the perceived benefit of research in respect of funding and by the leverage research exerts on league tables... the second is the time that is likely to be taken for the proposals to deliver the anticipated benefits.'

There is a third dimension: finding the energy, structures and resource to stimulate fundamental and lasting change across the whole institution. We concentrated on the educational experience in the first year. This may cause retention problems later on if the revamped educational experience in the first year fails to prepare students for what comes next. Learning, teaching and assessment (LTA) approaches must be developmental and coherent over the lifetime of the programme. On reflection, it may be preferable to review the need for changes in LTA approach programme by programme rather than by year of study.

Our audit led us to a greater emphasis on transformational strategies. The balance of activity has moved away from the SRP to other central departments (Educational Development, Life Long Learning, Student Support, Registry, Corporate Services and so on) and, importantly, from the administrative centre to the faculties and schools (although heavily supported by the centre). This broadening out of responsibility and scope reflects the maturity of Napier's efforts to address retention, and the extent to which retention thinking has slowly become embedded.

Napier's long-term efforts to improve retention, together with our experience of the work of other institutions, have helped us see which retention strategies are and aren't likely to work, and whether institutions are likely to improve retention by accident or design. We have come to see that transformational change is the key to effecting fundamental cultural change and sustainable improvements in retention.

But how to avoid the pitfalls of what doesn't work? Every HE institution is different. Retention strategies will be affected by the university's context, student characteristics and staff culture. There are no guaranteed solutions, but our experience has identified some common mistakes:

- **Trying everything to see what works.** The effect is often to dissipate resource and impetus, and to keep individual initiatives small-scale.

Also, it may promote conflicting initiatives and send conflicting messages to staff about priorities.

- **Assuming that good practice spreads organically.** Many retention projects start with an audit of work currently being undertaken by the faculties to improve retention. This will identify a range of good practice, often carried out by individuals in isolated pockets, which is then brought together and disseminated to staff in the form of a report. This rarely results in any good practice being picked up and embedded outside the home department.

- **Focusing primarily on student support issues.** Retention projects are often sited within student services departments, or led by guidance tutors. This can lead to overemphasizing student support issues – particularly student finance – as the key to improving retention. Other equally important areas, such as curriculum and methods for learning, teaching and assessment, may be neglected. Also, how far do the minority of students who actually use student services represent the broader student constituency?

- **Assuming that caring staff are enough to get the job done.** Staff are genuinely concerned about students. However, many of their decisions about how to shape the student experience are based on gut feeling rather than hard evidence. Students who drop out are more likely to leave without saying why. Vocal complainers are more likely to stay. So staff perceptions of the range of student concerns may be distorted by what students say rather than what they do.

- **Restricting research to 'drop-outs' or to one-off projects.** Students who withdraw are remarkably similar to those who stay. The factors that influence retention vary over time, following changes in the student body. For example, mature students at Napier are highly successful some years, and not in others. Strategies based on snapshots will inevitably be flawed.

- **Assuming that the work can be led at faculty or department level.** Faculties often argue that their students are inherently different from those in other faculties, and so they should be entirely free to address student retention problems in their own way. Certainly some work must be done locally, but allowing complete freedom inevitably leads to unacceptable variation in the student experience. The balance between the centre and the faculties is very important, and difficult to achieve.

We are still learning what measures are effective in improving student retention. Our reflections on progress in five years' time will no doubt yield a new set of considerations, and yet more adjustments. Many students were failing to progress for reasons totally unrelated to maintaining standards. By looking at programme delivery, support mechanisms and making student retention an important issue, we have significantly raised our progression rates. However, we have not lowered standards. Napier accepts that a combination of widening access and maintaining standards will inevitably lead to a lower progression rate than that of institutions who are highly selective if no other steps are taken. We seek a situation where no student fails who has the academic capacity to succeed. By dealing with the problem from this viewpoint, we have made considerable progress.

References

Beatty-Guenter, P (1994) Sorting, supporting, connecting and transforming: retention strategies at community colleges, *Community College Journal of Research*, **18** (2), pp 113–29

Yorke, M (1999) *Leaving Early: Undergraduate non-completion in higher education*, Falmer Press, London

CHAPTER 14

STANDING OUT IN A BIG CROWD

Case reporter: Steve Outram

Issues raised

The issues raised in this case are how a university can make itself distinctive, and how to make a top-down initiative work throughout a university.

Background

In the middle of the 1990s, Staffordshire University in the UK recognized that it needed a different approach to planning its future. The university had a distinctive reputation neither for research nor for teaching. The situation was not grave, but it was not going to get better of its own accord. The case reporter, the head of educational development, was heavily involved from the start in devising and then implementing the university's plans for improvement.

PART 1

Autumn 1995: the government had announced its public sector funding plans. These included reductions in the per capita fees income that universities would receive. Professor King, vice-chancellor of Staffordshire University, met with her deputy vice-chancellors and looked into the future. The results of their deliberations were stark. Within two or three years the university would have serious funding difficulties. Cost-cutting alone was not the solution, whatever unpleasant form that might take – reductions in staffing, higher student/staff ratios and so on. The university senior staff instead took the chance to reflect about Staffordshire University's identity and purpose as a higher education institution.

It was clear to most of us what we were not. We were not a highly regarded research university. We were ranked 140th, that is close to the bottom, in the 1992 Higher Education Funding Council Research Assessment Exercise. Neither were we famous for the quality or innovativeness of our teaching. We had achieved no 'excellent' gradings from the Teaching Quality Assessments undertaken so far by the Funding Council. We did not have a distinctive reputation for any particular area of learning and teaching – we were not, for example, a pioneer in work-based learning, or a recognized centre of expertise in learning technology. UK higher education is a big, competitive crowd.

What could we do to stand out that was truthful and realistic? This was my challenge as head of educational development. I could squirrel myself away in my office and dream up all manner of (possibly) brilliant solutions; but I knew that wasn't the way. I knew the university had to invent its own way forward if it was to own and implement its future with heart and head. So I worked with senior staff to plan, not an outcome, but a process.

In May 1996, senior staff and representatives from the trade unions and Student Union spent two days away from the university. We worked together to discover whether the view that change was needed was shared more widely; and if it was, what future direction we should take. At my suggestion, the event was facilitated by external development consultants with a national and international reputation for managing change in higher education. My role was to liaise between the various different staff and groups and with the consultants.

I had my doubts about using external consultants, however capable they were. Could they tune in quickly enough to the particular character of our university, or would their previous experience and expectation get in the way? And would the university in turn open up enough to outsiders? Senior staff, particularly those with research aspirations, were not keen to have the facts of the institution's research record or its learning and teaching record presented critically.

These doubts evaporated very quickly once we started to address the critical issues. As I had hoped, the external consultants could and did say things, and said them in direct ways, that I would have struggled with if I wanted to maintain good working relationships with my senior colleagues. And I was acutely conscious that I would need to maintain these good relationships with senior colleagues if I was to have any chance of working with them to implement whatever we came up with!

What the consultants saw, and what those present could readily sign up to, was the view of the university as a learning community; a place which valued collaboration and peer support, a place where people (mostly) felt they belonged and were welcome, a place that (mostly) made new arrivals feel welcome and included. The idea, and then the name, that emerged for the proposed new institutional learning and teaching strategy was 'Building a Learning Community', now known across the university as BLC. The idea and the name have proved powerful.

Of course we needed the vice chancellor's support. Throughout the two days when the strategy was drafted, she made it very clear that she would support a new learning and teaching strategy that was student focused. She would ensure that the strategy was resourced and neither student-centredness nor adequate resourcing was negotiable. Her support endured throughout the years during which the draft strategy was discussed, firmed and implemented across the university.

We also needed support from the executive, especially when we met resistance from senior staff including some deans and associate deans. As is common at such times, a small number of senior colleagues found that they could not support the new learning and teaching strategy and the importance it was being given. They voluntarily left the university, gaining posts in other universities, retiring or going into other forms of employment.

Following the creation of the draft learning and teaching strategy, all the academic schools in the university had their own 'away-day' events, also facilitated by the external consultants. The brief for these events was for each school to make its own particular interpretation of the overall strategy. All schools were required to suggest ways in which they might progress the strategy. 'Think institutionally, act locally.'

Crucially, each school had to show how it would create space and find time to develop and implement new ways of learning and teaching. A new university committee provided a place where school responses to, and plans to implement, the strategy could be discussed. This new committee approved school plans, and each school received a modest amount of money to implement its plans following approval.

In the early stages, some colleagues saw creating space and finding time as the whole strategy! Others, as is the way of academics facing externally prompted change, protested, 'I'm already doing all this. What else do you expect me to do?' Still others said (to me) 'It's just another fad' and (to each other) 'If we keep quiet it will go away.'

Launching a bright idea is one thing, even with wide (though not universal) support, even with top management fully on side. But, as resistance emerged, I began to seriously wonder if I had the energy and the skills to sustain what was clearly going to take several years.

How can you ensure wide ownership of a top-down initiative?
How can you deal with resistance to new strategies?
How can developers sustain energy for long-term projects?

PART 2

We addressed resistance in a number of ways. I worked with staff at all levels to promote wider ownership of the strategy. I played 'bad cop', stressing again and again that the university had decided to proceed in this way. I also played 'good cop', offering advice and help and modest resources to help people plan how they would implement the strategy. Please don't ask me which role I preferred or was best at!

All schools were asked to suggest amendments to the text of the strategy. We ran staff development events centrally in the university as well as within schools. We consulted groups of staff. We welcomed private comments from individuals, and took them seriously. We ran regular meetings with deans and associate deans. I routinely briefed the senior management team on progress, and made suggestions for future action. In all, nine versions of the strategy were drafted and discussed across the university before the final version was formally agreed at Academic Board in 1998, two years after we had started the quest. That was a great day!

To support the implementation of the strategy and ensure the new learning and teaching strategy was adopted across the whole university and not just by those colleagues who were enthusiastic for change, we top-sliced existing school budgets. A proportion of funds was allocated to schools to support their action plans as approved by the Learning and Teaching Committee. And a smaller proportion of funds was allocated on the basis of competitive bidding in which criteria based on the strategy were used to evaluate project submissions. This ensured that the initiative reached right across the campus, and allowed us to identify and support champions. Action plans and criterion-referenced project funding meant that colleagues were all doing things that were in broad alignment.

In subsequent years we stopped allocating project funds via competitive bidding. Instead, we used some funds to support central initiatives identified as a priority, and allocated the rest to schools according to their student enrolments. This way, we no longer had to spend time on managing a competitive scheme that included giving feedback to disappointed bidders. We avoided the political flak from schools that were less successful in their bidding – especially those that submitted elegant research proposals rather than learning and teaching development and innovation proposals! Each year, we agreed central priorities, and built these into the annual operating statement of the university. This also gave me and my educational development team a clear agenda, and authority, for our work.

Local support and local contact were vital. We asked each school to identify a person to be a project manager, responsible for implementing the strategy in their school. I chaired and supported the group of school project managers. This expert group became a strong lever for achieving the goals of the strategy, and also helped the university to become a place where talking about learning and teaching was important and valued.

As we became more experienced in what we were doing, we increasingly utilized project management tools. In particular we used the logical framework of LogFrame, a project management system used successfully by colleagues in one of the schools, based on their European Commission and World Bank funded projects. We now ask all schools to submit their plans for implementing the strategy using the LogFrame template. Figure 14.1 (at the end) shows the questions that this template asks.

Perhaps inevitably initiative fatigue was beginning to set in, and not just with the educational development team! And some of the innovation process itself was starting to feel rather routine. So we still faced questions.

What do you do to make and keep a learning and teaching strategy distinctive?
How do you join a learning and teaching strategy up with other institutional strategies?
How can you keep colleagues energized and looking forward?

PART 3

To keep innovation alive, and to make the learning and teaching strategy still more appropriately distinctive, the university decided in 1998 to adopt and use a proprietary virtual learning environment (VLE). We made this work by following the same principles we had already established in developing the learning and teaching strategy. A small group of 'champions' was carefully selected to be early adopters.

We also followed this practice in other areas of learning and teaching strategy. For example we identified 'champions' for the introduction of personal development planning (PDP) across the curriculum, and for the wider use of accreditation of prior (experiential) learning (AP(E)L) across the campus. Each early adopter was given a significant amount of training, and, where appropriate, access to external experts. Funds were made available to schools (and to some central services) to support the early adopters, following receipt and agreement of an action plan. Clear milestones and deadlines were identified, and met. There was support in a structure and with accountability.

It may sound so far as if Building a Learning Community has been a wholly academic initiative. It started that way. But very early on, we realized that we had to integrate the institutional learning and teaching strategy with other university strategies, and that meant we had to work with support staff and services. This in turn meant that some university services also undertook projects as a part of the Building a Learning Community initiative. For example:

- The Estates Strategy concentrated on developing the appropriate classroom specification for delivering the learning and teaching strategy.

- The Personnel Strategy was developed to include a Learning and Teaching Fellowship scheme to reward excellent tutors.
- The Library and Information Services Strategy was developed in a number of ways to support the learning and teaching strategy, including the development of an Information Skills module, to be taken by all students.
- The Research Strategy was developed to include pedagogic research and development and the creation of a new research centre with a focus on higher education innovation.
- The Student Office was solidly engaged with the learning and teaching strategy. It helped develop the student transcript and the inclusion of PDP (personal development planning) within the curriculum. One of the outcomes was the development of a Career Planning module delivered to a variety of awards.
- The Information Technology strategy was integrated with the learning and teaching strategy. One positive outcome of this alignment was the explicit identification of service standards and equipment specification standards as well as a clear and focused spending programme.
- With colleagues, I developed guidelines and a process of quality assuring online learning in association with the University Quality Improvement Service.

Having 'joined-up' strategies is important, but so is knowing which strategy is the driver – the one that all the others support or follow. Undoubtedly, from 1998 until 2002, the institutional learning and teaching strategy, Building a Learning Community, together with the university's widening participation strategy, drove the university's purpose and activities.

What do you think of the overall approach to developing and implementing a learning and teaching strategy?
Could the approach be applied in your institution? What difficulties might there be?

CASE REPORTER'S DISCUSSION

There is no doubt that Building a Learning Community has been successful. At an institutional level, the university has gained a distinctive reputation for its learning and teaching developments and for its associated VLE work. Since the formal adoption of BLC in 1998, all nine subjects that have had external Quality Assurance Agency subject reviews have achieved 'excellent' scores. The BLC strategy was commended by the Quality Assurance Agency in 2001:

The team concluded that the BLC initiative has provided the University with the core of a distinctive learning and teaching strategy which is valued by both staff and students. The University is to be commended for this initiative.
(Quality Assurance Agency for Higher Education, Staffordshire University, Quality Audit Report, November 2001, para. 75)

The university has been much more successful in bidding for funds for learning and teaching projects, and several members of staff have been very successful in gaining recognition as learning and teaching experts. But if we were to start again we would do a number of things differently.

First, we would evaluate the effectiveness of strategy and policy changes from the outset, using university-wide formative evaluation instruments. Second, we would recognize that some staff will remain doubters to the end. Rather than spend lots of time trying to convince this minority to change, it is better to work to achieve early success.

Third, we would recognize that it is vital to have maximum clarity of result and purpose, and to keep revisiting that purpose – not just introduce change for change's sake, and jeopardize the success of the initiative. Fourth, from the start we would explain what is happening, as effectively and as widely as possible. We didn't do this, and a number of colleagues got the wrong message. We then had to spend a lot of time clarifying the strategy and otherwise reassuring colleagues.

We still have more work to do in effectively disseminating the strategy, both for understanding and for use. We are pretty sure that, by now, the vast majority of staff at the university know at least something about Building a Learning Community. But still, not all of them necessarily fully understand it. And certainly some are still not fully exploiting and supporting it.

So what have we learned from Building a Learning Community about what makes an institutional learning and teaching strategy work? What advice would we offer?

- Agree what the starting problem or circumstance is.
- Negotiate and agree a clear vision.
- Translate this vision into the results that you wish to achieve.
- Say why you wish to achieve these results.
- Allow people time and space to make their own sense of the strategy.
- Encourage schools and courses to develop their own plans for local implementation.
- Stay committed to the strategy.
- Provide resources for policy-related developments and initiatives.
- Ensure clear authority and support at the most senior levels.
- Give people permission to try and fail.
- Develop an expert group.

- Provide spaces where it is legitimate, indeed encouraged, to talk about learning and teaching.
- Use project management resources.
- Cost accurately.
- Agree clear targets, linked to milestones and deadlines.
- Ensure good communications and dissemination systems.
- Work hard for early successes, and reward these.
- Join up with other strategies, and be clear which strategy is the driver.
- Evaluate from the outset.
- Review the strategy to keep it alive.
- Use all of the political and analytical skills associated with being a good change manager.

Figure 14.1   Institutional Learning and Teaching Strategy Projects (BLC) 2000–2001: template for a project proposal

School/Service:

Project Title:

Narrative Summary	Verifiable Indicators	Means of Verification	Assumptions
Goal			
Which aspect of *Building a Learning Community* or the university's corporate plan does this project relate to?	How can you verify that this project contributes to achieving a wider impact and meets identified needs, eg in what way does this project have a cross-university impact?	What information exists outside your project that will help you provide evidence of the impact of your project, eg student employability; QAA reports?	What external assumptions and conditions relate to this project and what conditions are necessary for the sustainability of the project, eg what external contingencies need to be taken into account?
Purpose			
What is the rationale for the project? How will students benefit? What will be the overall impact on them?	How will you judge whether you have been successful/effective from the student's point of view, eg improved examination results; higher student satisfaction; better results with less class contact; higher student numbers?	What external baseline information exists in relation to this project, eg comparison with other universities? How strong is external information in relation to this project, eg comparison of use of different VLEs; external evaluation of distributed learning?	What assumptions or conditions might create barriers to meeting the goals and rationale of the project, eg is your project ambitious enough; will you be able to deliver entirely off-campus? Where might there be resistance to the project?
Outcomes/outputs			
What are the expected outcomes from this project?	Do you have clear milestones for achievement? How many? When? Where? Who?	How will you gain feedback and evaluate the achievement of the outcomes?	Are you confident that your desired outcomes will achieve the purpose? Are there any outcomes that are dependent on external risks or threats, eg do any of your outcomes rely on support from outside your school or service?
Activities			
What activities will you carry out in order that the outcomes will be achieved? How will the outcomes be disseminated? What plans are there to inform your appropriate LTSN?	What are the resource inputs into this project (financial and human) and how will you work with the LDC on this project? Eg overall, how much of your BLC funds will be spent on this project and in what ways?	How will you measure and monitor resource use?	Do you have sufficient resources to achieve your outputs/ outcomes? What resources do you have now; do you need to appoint new staff?

CHAPTER 15

TOO MUCH TOO SOON?

Case reporter: Roger Landbeck

Issue raised

The issue raised in this case is how to introduce changes in policies and procedures in order to improve teaching and learning.

Background

This case occurred in the 1990s in a small university in a developing country. The case reporter had been appointed director of a new centre that was to provide both staff development and learning assistance to students, particularly in the areas of English and Mathematics. Previously, he had worked for 18 years in an academic development unit in Australia.

PART 1

I sat in the small office, which was my temporary home in the university. The heavy wooden louvered door allowed the ceiling fan to draw in some breeze to alleviate the hot, steamy tropical day. Outside was the beautiful campus full of lush tropical plants, where the students were busily getting themselves organized for the new academic year. It was my first day as director of a new centre established to provide staff development and learning assistance to students. Learning assistance had been offered for some years previously through the English and Mathematics departments. Staff development as practised in Australian universities was, by contrast, an unknown quantity.

What a great opportunity to make a positive impact on teaching and learning. How was I going to use it? I had a real desire to achieve something worthwhile as the new director but coupled with it, anxiety at the possibility of failure.

My first few weeks were marked by professional loneliness heightened by adjusting to life in a new culture away from my familiar world. My two colleagues were skilled in their field but had no experience in staff development, nor were they familiar with the literature. Staff in the Department of Education, who were housed in the same building, were not familiar with research in higher education. So it was difficult for me to share ideas with colleagues as I had done in Australia. All of this reminded me that if the centre was going to make an impact for good in the university then I was going to have to do it. This for me was quite a scary prospect!

I needed to get out and meet academics, both to outline what I thought the centre would try to do, and to hear what they were doing in research. So in the first few months I met staff in a series of departmental meetings. On reflection, what was interesting about the meetings was the greater interest in what the centre could do to improve student performance compared with my ideas on staff development. This role of the centre – to assist students – had become familiar to them through the work of my colleagues before I arrived. Thus the concept of staff development would take time to establish.

I ran a series of seminars on teaching and learning to help staff become familiar with research in this area. One of the seminars was on student learning, and afterwards a lecturer in linguistics asked me if I would be interested in a project to investigate how students learnt in her class. Of course I was delighted, and thus began a five-year collaborative research project, which provided me with the most stimulating professional contact I have experienced. It also provided data about students, which I believed was a useful way to help staff examine their teaching in a less threatening manner.

My previous experience in Australia showed me the value of being represented on the strategic policy-making committees of the university, so I was encouraged that quite soon after I arrived, the VC agreed to put me on the Academic Committee, Senate and all three school boards of study. However, I was not successful in persuading him about membership of the Staff Review Committee, where I could see there would be a useful role in influencing the policy on staff performance. Through being a member of these committees I was also able to gain a university-wide view of issues, and had the opportunity of becoming visible to fellow academics and making useful contributions to the debates. All of this was very positive. I had no way of knowing what lay ahead.

An unsatisfactory course evaluation system provided me with an opportunity to make changes to policies and procedures. I began working on the package, which I hoped would replace the existing system early in my second year at the university.

The existing system consisted of a closed questionnaire containing about 30 questions about the course and the teaching of the course, which was administered to students during the last lecture of the course. It was compulsory for all undergraduate courses. The questionnaires were sent to the academic secretariat for processing, and the results were sent to the staff member. Unfortunately this processing was not a high priority for a hard-pressed secretariat, and it emerged that many staff had never received any results of the surveys, which made them quite useless. I also felt that several of the questions were quite inappropriate.

My proposal for change was to provide staff with a package containing a discussion of the nature of evaluation and a variety of methods that they could use. The emphasis was on getting staff to take responsibility for their own evaluation and thereby free them from reliance on a central system. I needed to negotiate approval for this change through the administrative layers of school boards of studies on to the Academic Committee and then Senate. Our centre was represented at each stage of the process.

The proposal to replace the existing course evaluation system with the package was accepted by the school boards without much discussion, but it became evident that the concept of evaluation was not understood. Even when it was stressed repeatedly that evaluation is more than questionnaires, the discussion dropped back into details of questionnaires. That should have been a warning of the difficulty of changing conceptions of evaluation.

There was another important factor that I did not sufficiently appreciate at first. If the package was accepted it would effectively end the compulsory evaluation of all courses, because staff would be free to design their own evaluation and carry it out when they wished. The result was that it would no longer be possible to monitor the quality of teaching.

So when the package was discussed at the Academic Committee it was not surprising that several members were not prepared to give this up. Nonetheless, I was encouraged by the general support for the package, until Bill from Science spoke up. 'I suggest we allow the staff to use the package if they wish as an alternative to the current system, which we will retain. But since there are problems with the analysis of the closed questions I suggest we don't bother to do the analysis anymore.' Bill was quite influential and had previously chaired the committee. It began to look that this suggestion would be passed.

Suddenly my mind was racing as an alarming prospect was looming. Sure the staff could use the package if they wished *but* the worst feature was that the unsatisfactory questionnaire was being retained! I was stunned – so stunned in fact that I said nothing. I could hardly believe how quickly things could change through a single contribution. Was all the effort to introduce an improved system to be for nothing? I had hoped to get rid of the old completely and replace it with the new system. Had this been too much too soon? Could the situation be rescued?

What would you have done if you had been in the meeting?
What other action could be taken to rescue the situation?

PART 2

During the meeting I was too stunned to mount a rational argument about the consequences of the decision that was being made. Afterwards, however, I had time to reflect on what had happened and realized that there would be an opportunity to retrieve the situation at the next meeting of the Academic Committee. I decided to raise two points: First, if the closed questions were no longer to be analysed then there would be little point in getting students to fill in the questionnaires. Second, I proposed to replace the 'unsatisfactory' closed questionnaire with a four-item open questionnaire focusing on the course, which I argued would give much superior information to the existing instrument.

In proposing the new questionnaire I was prepared to lose the original objective of introducing the package in order to achieve some improvement to the system. In the event the Academic Committee and subsequently the Senate accepted my arguments, and the simple questionnaire was put into practice. Lecturers received the set of questionnaires back after the assessment period, and were able to carry out the analysis themselves.

To my knowledge the course evaluation package was never used; in fact there was more interest in it from other universities! However, the discussions at the different committees provided some useful feedback on the draft package, and it became obvious that the original version was far too detailed and lengthy. I therefore revised the package and circulated parts of it as single-sheet papers on evaluation, which seemed a useful way of disseminating new ideas.

The experience brought home very clearly the value of being represented on strategic committees. Because I was present at the crucial decision about the package I was able to retrieve the situation.

What factors need to be considered when introducing a teaching and learning innovation?
If you were appointed director of a new staff development centre, what would you do?

CASE REPORTER'S DISCUSSION

So was it 'too much too soon'? Yes, and one aspect of this was my failure to have enough close contact with teaching staff to be able to appreciate their concerns, the pressures under which they worked, and their conceptions of teaching and learning. If I had appreciated these factors, I might have made more realistic proposals for change. In this case perhaps I took insufficient account of what was possible in the situation. However, others may argue that 'who dares wins'. Sometimes we need to aim high in order to make a greater gain.

A further point was my failure to respect the level of expertise of the staff and invite them to share this. Fortunately during my last two years in the centre, this changed and some fruitful cooperation occurred between the centre and the teaching staff. Had I appreciated this expertise in my early days, I would have felt far less lonely professionally.

One of the most successful outcomes of this recognition was the production of a small publication called *Hints for Teachers* – a collection of the great variety of experiences of teaching contributed by 30 academics. This proved of great value for staff new to the culture both of the university and the country.

The situation of being director in a new centre brought about a desire to achieve some useful outcomes, coupled with the anxiety about possible failure. Thus I had a strong personal agenda, driven by conceptions of staff development built up elsewhere over a number of years. The question arises, was this personal agenda matched to that of the university in establishing the centre? What if the university needed to become aware of new possibilities of staff development? Should the developer push ahead with his/her agenda and try to lead the university into new directions?

It is vital for developers to understand the nature of the environment in which they are working. Often the developers' agenda requires conceptual change, and often this is very slow to occur. Nevertheless, as research in teaching and learning has shown, conceptual change is most likely to be of lasting effect. Unfortunately today's economic climate does not encourage slow change; there is a demand for results. Inevitably, compromise is needed, as occurred with the course evaluation package.

My experiences with introducing changes to policy and procedures in the years following the incident with the course evaluation package were quite different and more productive. While it is possible that one reason for differences was that I was becoming more accepted by the academic community, I believe the major reason for the change was the support given to me and the centre by the deputy vice-chancellor and the pro vice-chancellor (academic), both of whom were local academics.

For example, the pro vice-chancellor (academic) was chair of the Academic Committee, and often he would refer problems about teaching and learning to me during the meetings to provide discussion papers for the committee. These provided opportunities to be part of a team and to influence policy and procedures in a way that would have been impossible had I not been a member of the committee. One good example was the introduction of a staff appraisal system.

So what can staff developers learn about introducing change from this case? Briefly the need to:

- know the academic staff well and respect their expertise;
- be prepared to 'cut your cloth' according to the local situation;

- work with the overall vision of the university to assist it to achieve its goals, but also at times be prepared to offer alternative visions if this will result in improved teaching and learning.

However, perhaps most of all the case study demonstrates the value of having a voice on strategic decision-making committees and gaining the support of academics in positions of influence. This makes it more possible to achieve significant positive changes in policies relating to teaching and learning.

CHAPTER 16

WE'RE NOT LAUGHING NOW

Case reporters: Sylvia Huntley-Moore and John Panter

Issues raised

This case raises issues in the introduction of staff and academic development to a traditional collegiate university. The issues include institutional culture, location of activities, focus, strategies and long-term survival.

Background

In 1995, Sylvia moved from a relatively new corporate-style Australian university with an established system of centralized planning, clear structures and well-integrated staff and academic development functions to a 400-year-old prestigious collegiate university in Ireland, to take up the new post of staff development officer. The post was an administrative one, and Sylvia was located in the Personnel Office.

Previously, Sylvia had been employed in an academic development unit where her primary role was teaching development, with a particular emphasis on the use of student evaluation to improve teaching.

PART 1

As I left the dark leather and polished wood of the Senior Common Room and walked back to my office across the cobbled square, I thought about my colleague's parting comment, 'When you came here, we thought staff development was a joke, not to mention the idea that someone could tell us about teaching. Well, we're not laughing now.'

This comment sent me back to my first day in the new job, as I sat alone in my office wondering where to start. I pored over my job description, hoping for inspiration. Unfortunately this only reinforced the enormity of my brief. How was I (with no additional support) going to identify the training needs of all college staff and provide them with training packages, while maintaining close links with staff development activities in other universities and sourcing external funding? And what was this preoccupation with training all about?

My first year in college passed in a flurry of activity. With barely two months between my arrival and the start of the academic year, I was under pressure to produce and distribute a booklet of staff development workshops for the coming year. With no time to spare I devised titles and brief outlines for 14 workshops on a variety of topics related to teaching and management.

When the application forms came flooding in I was greatly relieved but also daunted. Rightly or not, I felt my credibility was on the line, as well as the college's future acceptance of staff development. I simply had to make the first year's programme a success. With these thoughts in mind I was kept busy designing and running teaching development workshops, as well as locating and briefing management consultants.

I spent a lot of time worrying. Would the programme meet staff needs? Had it been a big mistake to think I could do this? At times I felt very isolated and alone, but I have to admit that the buzz from the first successful workshop was a great motivator and confidence-booster.

A few of the staff I met through workshops invited me to their departments to talk about teaching issues, and on several occasions I was invited back to run workshops on topics of particular interest to them. I really enjoyed the experience of being out there in the 'real world', working as part of an enthusiastic and committed team.

At some point during that first year I found time to think about a training needs analysis. With 64 academic departments I decided to focus on the six faculty executives (consisting of a dean and associated heads of department) as my primary sources of information, and hopefully future champions of academic development. I simply didn't have time to get to the administrative and support units yet.

The six deans invited me to address their executives. This was a positive sign, I thought. At least they were prepared to see me! On the other hand, having no idea what to expect I felt quite nervous. Nevertheless, I attended my first meeting with high hopes. This was a great opportunity to get the deans and heads on-side, and I intended to introduce them to my vision for academic development – which involved more than training packages!

At the conclusion of my last presentation I looked around the room expectantly, only to be met with polite silence and glazed expressions. And with a few memorable exceptions, this was the response from each of the faculty executives. Among the memorable exceptions was the head who pointed his finger at me accusingly and said, 'If it wasn't for your appointment I could have had two new lecturers.' Another was the head who, smiling at me with genuine warmth, said, 'At last, I can be trained properly in how to use an overhead projector!' This comment was probably the most disheartening!

Faced with this lack of support, what would you do next?

PART 2

I was disappointed and shaken by the experience with the faculty executives. Clearly they weren't going to be the champions I'd hoped. So I was back to square one with the needs analysis, and feeling rather unsure of myself and of my role in the college. If these relatively senior academics couldn't see what I was talking about, then maybe I should limit my sights to overhead projector training.

Around this time, much to my relief, I found that the workshop evaluation sheets provided a rich source of ideas for future planning, and for the short term at least I decided they would constitute my training needs analysis.

The evaluation sheets also provided an outlet for staff concerns and frustrations. The most frequent ones were 'Why isn't my head of department/manager doing this course?', 'This is a waste of time unless the promotions system values teaching!', and 'Support staff need career paths and promotion opportunities.' These types of issue were often raised in workshops too, and it was during one of these quite heated discussions that it dawned on me. My colleagues expected the staff development officer to be their advocate.

Fired up by my colleagues' expectations and fed up with the negative effect these issues were having on staff development, I decided to see what I could do about them. My first port of call was the personnel manager, my immediate boss. He was most understanding and promptly invited me to join a working party reviewing career paths and promotions for administrative and support staff.

Unfortunately, the issue of academic promotions wasn't quite so easily addressed. As an administrator based in the Personnel Office I didn't have direct access to senior academics, nor was I included on the committees that dealt with such matters. When I did manage finally to raise the issue informally with a senior academic, his response was a look of disbelief that this could be an issue, given that the procedures had just been revised.

Shortly after this, I was invited to present a report to the college's Personnel Committee (comprising senior academic and non-academic staff) on the first year of staff and academic development activities. I decided to use this opportunity to have another shot at raising these issues, as well as supplying statistics on workshop attendance. They warmly received my report but ignored the issues, their only recommendations being that I should offer a management development programme for senior administrators and another for heads of academic departments – not a view necessarily shared by the heads themselves!

I left the committee meeting feeling incredibly frustrated at their failure to address the issues I'd raised, but also greatly relieved to know that, at least in their eyes, the first staff development programme had been a success and I wasn't going to be asked to pack my bags – just yet!

Given this further setback, what other courses of action are there?
How is the location of staff development within Personnel affecting the situation?

PART 3

I couldn't think of anything more to do about the issues raised with the Personnel Committee, so I focused my energies on building the staff development programme to meet as many of my colleagues' immediate needs as possible. Each year from 1996–2000 the programme grew, with new courses in teaching, management, personal effectiveness and quality improvement.

I spent a lot of time designing new courses, but this meant that the programme attracted and kept a growing cadre of enthusiastic academics, many of whom helped to initiate change in their own departments. Very often these academics came to me for support and guidance, and many happy hours were spent drinking coffee and discussing their plans for improving teaching, and as well as their frustrations in trying to bring about change in their departments.

It was time-consuming and difficult to see immediate results, but there was great satisfaction in hearing how a colleague eventually managed to initiate curricular discussion in a department where they admitted, 'We've never talked to each other about teaching in 20 years. This is very interesting. Let's keep doing it.' A few colleagues went so far as conducting research into their teaching that was subsequently published.

Not all of their experiences, however, were so productive. In some instances departmental culture and tradition was extremely resistant, and in these cases I was their only ally, but I had to be careful not to push them too far and too soon, in case they gave up all together. It really was like walking a tightrope, and sometimes I felt drained and wondered if the time spent was worth the effort. Indeed I was tempted occasionally to take their hands, look into their eyes and say, 'For the sake of your own career, forget all this and concentrate on your research.'

Happily, not all departmental cultures were so resistant to change, and I found myself working more frequently with those departments that saw the need for systematic curricular change, strategic planning, and, most often, training for their postgraduate teaching assistants.

Despite my having made some impact in the area of teaching development, staff development generally was still very much seen as training for individuals, and there were still huge unmet development needs for support staff. On a professional level, I often felt alone in the college and indeed in the country. Only one other university had employed a full-time academic developer, and staff development generally was handled on a part-time basis by personnel staff whose major role was to employ external consultants to conduct training.

Since I had worked in a substantial academic centre in Australia with the support of a well-established professional network, I found it very difficult to sustain the energy levels required to do the job in the way I wanted. Sometimes I felt completely overwhelmed by the task, but I couldn't afford to let this show to my colleagues who looked to me for support and encouragement. Towards the end of 1997 all this came to a head, and I was seriously thinking of returning to Australia.

Fortunately my previous boss (John), a senior academic, had recently retired, and taking advantage of the situation, I found the money to offer him a contract post as academic developer. Much to my relief he agreed to come to Ireland, so finally I had someone 'to talk shop with'. The importance of shared language and experience can't be overestimated, and given his status as a retired academic, no head of department would think of him as a 'mere administrator'! From a personal point of view his appointment gave me a renewed impetus, and professionally we were able to enrich and diversify the programme.

John's arrival gave me more time to think about development for administrative and support staff, but still not enough time or resources to conduct a formal analysis of their needs. In this instance, however, being part of the Personnel Office was a real advantage. It gave me easy access to the industrial relations people, and through them to representatives of the relevant unions. It was really refreshing to talk about staff development with groups of people who were enthusiastic and who had the formal power to support my efforts. As a result of these discussions we began to introduce development activities to meet the particular needs of groups such as secretaries, supervisors and technical team leaders.

Having at least partially dealt with the cause of my own stress, I began to notice significant growth in enrolments for stress management courses. Indeed it proved necessary to double the number of advertised courses and to provide follow-up sessions. The overwhelming response to these courses was very positive, but they uncovered a range of issues including poor communications and insufficient training for heads of department, managers and supervisors.

Spurred on by this feedback I introduced programmes for heads of department and managers. I tried to do all the right things, starting with a needs analysis covering content, format and timing. Both groups indicated that they wanted a series of short inputs on specific issues from external management experts. I spent ages tracking down Ireland's most esteemed management development experts, only to find that both heads and managers were highly critical of the programme because the experts 'failed to understand the college context'. The only session rated highly by the participants was one in which John spoke about his experience as a head of department.

This result was particularly galling. I'd done a systematic needs analysis and followed it through by producing the programme the target groups said they wanted rather than the one I thought they needed, and the result was disaster. This was my big chance to get significant numbers of heads and managers directly involved, but in the end most of them were turned off. During the final plenary session the only thing that the heads as a group were positive about was the opportunity they had had to meet each other. Trying to salvage something good out of the whole mess, I decided to provide a venue for them to meet informally two or three times a year. I also host a one-day induction course for newly appointed heads, but attempts to expand this have so far met with apathy.

From John's perspective, after many years working in a corporate-style university, he found the cultural differences exciting and challenging and occasionally amusing, as at the time when tasting wine in the college cellar, he was confronted by an even older academic. Peering at John's Trinity tie, he remarked, 'But you don't look like a college man.' John still isn't sure whether to take this remark as a compliment or an insult.

While I was busy working with administrative and support staff, John (in his 'spare' time) set about establishing closer links with the other Irish universities. By this stage there were still only two other academic developers in the Republic, although there were a number of enthusiastic academics who were happy to share their expertise.

It was following a meeting of this informal network that John returned to the college with the idea of holding Ireland's first national conference on higher education. Once the initial enthusiasm had worn off we did wonder what we'd let ourselves in for, but with lots of support and goodwill we pulled it off. Over 100 participants attended from all universities on the island, and we even managed to get the President of the Republic to give the opening address. The energy generated by this number of people coming together for the first time to share their experience of teaching was truly inspirational, and more than made up for my previous feelings of isolation – and I think those of a lot of other people too!

The conference ended in a plenary session where John proposed the formation of a society for higher education based on the Australian HERDSA model. His proposal was met with unanimous support and the All Ireland Society for Higher Education was launched a year later.

As John and I sat in our beautiful eighteenth-century office overlooking College Green contemplating the first summer holiday of the new millennium, we agreed that significant inroads had been made, particularly in the area of teaching development, and more generally that both academic and staff development were well established. As our colleague had said, 'They're not laughing now.'

What are the main messages that can be taken from this case?

CASE REPORTER'S DISCUSSION

Readers may wonder why, given my remit, I didn't set about a classical training needs analysis immediately on my appointment, especially as I was moving into a very different environment from the one I was used to. The reality of the situation was that my budget was wholly provided by a government agency that dictated the form and focus of the programme, as well as the primary target groups. As a result the programme consisted entirely of workshops, with a heavy emphasis on individual development primarily in relation to teaching.

I must admit that I probably would have chosen this course of action anyway. Offering a centralized workshop programme is an effective way of establishing a public presence for academic and staff development in a relatively short time. Given that teaching is a core function of the university and that the great majority of academics had no previous training in teaching, the immediate need was obvious and generic workshops were appropriate.

Conducting the workshops myself helped to build my credibility. This was absolutely vital given the location of the staff development function in a personnel office and my own formal status as 'an administrator'. The demarcation between what are perceived to be academic and administrative roles is often sharply drawn and guarded fiercely, particularly in traditional collegiate universities. This demarcation can pose specific problems for academic developers located in personnel offices who are expected to work closely with academics to improve teaching, which is quite clearly a core academic function. In other words, developers in such situations can be seen to be trespassing on academic territory.

On the other hand, in this instance the personnel staff were an invaluable source of support and information about college history, structures, policies and personalities, particularly in relation to the administrative and support staff.

It is our view that there is no easy answer to the problem of where to situate staff and academic development functions. One possible solution may be to situate administrative and support staff development in personnel offices, whereas academic development could be a part of the academic structure. The solution favoured by most Irish universities has been to situate staff development (including management development for academics) in personnel offices, with teaching development located in separate academic units.

A possible downside of this scenario is that 'administrators' are still partially responsible for the development of academics in their management role, and it remains unclear who, if anyone, should take a broader view of the developer's role in supporting, for example, strategic planning, and in influencing structural changes such as reform of promotions systems and the introduction of career development.

Neither the external funding body nor the senior staff of the college took the broader view. Staff and academic development was perceived purely as a matter of training for individuals. Yet in those early workshops significant numbers of these individuals perceived my role as being an advocate and agent for change as well as a trainer. It was on their initiative that I was able to start working at the departmental level, and thereby became involved in curriculum development and strategic planning.

Working directly with departments has proved very fruitful in bringing about change in perceptions of teaching and learning, and in teaching practice, but to date we have been able to influence only a few of them because of the prevailing view of staff development.

In the more corporate-style university we were used to, curriculum and strategic planning were conducted systematically, and the developer had a well-defined role in these processes. Thus institutional culture can limit or enable the scope of the developer's activities regardless of our models of best practice. In retrospect therefore it is not surprising that my naïve efforts to enlist the faculty executives as champions of a grand plan for refocusing academic and staff development met with little enthusiasm or understanding. Talk of departmental, faculty or institutional development was completely foreign to them.

On the whole, the faculty executives believed that teaching development was for newly appointed staff, for poor performers and for postgraduate teaching assistants. The focus was on improving lecturing methods of individual academics and assisting postgraduate teaching assistants to run their classes more efficiently. The idea of a collective approach to curriculum development was alien to most of them, teaching being in the main an individualistic and private concern. Unlike the UK and Australia, Ireland at that time had no system of quality audits, and compulsory departmental reviews were only introduced in 1999. Hence there was no external pressure for systematic review and development of teaching, and therefore no collective will to do it.

My fascination with the college culture led me to undertake some research into the perceived management development needs of newly appointed heads of department. I was not completely convinced by feedback that the first management development programme had failed simply because the external facilitators had not understood the college culture and context.

The research indicated that the heads were not a homogeneous group (although I had treated them as if they were) and that their perceptions of their management roles and their associated development needs were significantly influenced by their disciplinary backgrounds as well as, to a lesser extent, their gender and age. Of course having done this research I was left with the depressing prospect of having to provide quite different development options, at least for the various disciplinary groups, with only very limited resources. These findings may indicate why the literature on management development for heads of department reports so few examples of successful programmes.

The issue of resources, both human and financial, had a profound effect on the form and scope of the entire staff development programme. Perhaps my subconscious reason for not pursuing detailed needs analyses was the very real fear that by doing so I would raise expectations that could not be met. Though John's appointment provided the critical mass to keep expanding the academic development programme, it also meant there were fewer resources for administrative and support staff development, and to this day there are gaps, particularly with regard to technical staff development and funding for staff wishing to attend external courses.

I still wonder whether, given the funding situation and my particular expertise, I should have ignored my remit and concentrated on teaching development.

As this case is being written, the college is facing major changes in response to government legislation. The college's first strategic planning exercise is nearly complete, and this should result in the establishment of an agreed framework within which staff and academic development will operate. There is a proposal to establish a Centre for Academic Practice, which implies that academic staff development will no longer be located in the Personnel Office.

After a period of rapid growth the Irish economy has slowed, and this is reflected in significantly reduced funding for universities, which will probably lead to belt-tightening similar to that experienced in UK and Australian universities. In such a climate it is unlikely that the gaps in the staff development programme will be filled.

We live in interesting times.

Questions for personal reflection

- Where do you think staff and academic development units should be located in order to maximize their effectiveness?
- What do you think are legitimate roles for staff and academic developers?

SECTION 4

WORKING NATIONALLY

CHAPTER 17

FAR TOO SUCCESSFUL

Case reporter: David Baume

Issues raised

The issues raised in this case are coping with a success that threatens to damage your organization, and anticipating and providing what your members will need and want in a greatly changed environment.

Background

What is now SEDA, the UK Staff and Educational Development Association, started in the 1980s as an association for two main groups: staff and educational developers, and teaching and support staff who wanted to understand and improve teaching and learning. The organization produced a series of short publications on teaching and learning, and ran annual conferences. In 1992 SEDA launched a scheme to accredit teachers in higher education. The scheme was built on descriptions of the capabilities of higher education teachers, and of the values and principles that should underpin their practice. The scheme did not directly accredit individual teachers. Rather it reviewed programmes to train university teachers. It asked 'In order to pass this programme, does a lecturer have to demonstrate achievement of the SEDA capabilities underpinned by the SEDA values and principles?' If the answer was yes and a few more conditions were met then the programme was 'recognized', and those successfully completing it were 'accredited'. Programme recognition and review were undertaken by programme leaders trained for the role. Ten years later, some 2,500 teachers had been accredited and some 65 programmes recognized by SEDA, mainly in the UK but also in Australia, New Zealand, Hong Kong, Singapore and Sri Lanka.

Recognizing and reviewing these programmes generated a significant part of SEDA's activity and turnover. SEDA also developed other accreditation schemes, for example for higher education administrators.

The case reporter was elected chair of the association in 1990, and held the position for five years. He subsequently continued active involvement with the association.

PART 1

I was with the family on a narrow boat on the Brecon and Monmouth canal in South Wales in 1997. It was raining. At the appointed hour I used my shiny, and still rather magical, new mobile phone to ring Alison at the *Times Higher Education Supplement*.

'What does Dearing say about teacher accreditation?' I asked.

'He's recommended accreditation for all new teaching staff. He says nice things about the SEDA's work on teacher accreditation. There will be a new Institute to do this accreditation,' she reported. She read me the relevant sections of the report, then asked 'How does SEDA feel about all that?'

Rather like the newspaper editor in *Chicago*, with his two possible headlines already set up – 'Innocent!' and 'Guilty!' – I had prepared three possible responses. One was for if Dearing said yes to accreditation, one for if he said no, and one for if he said little or nothing about it. I ran through my 'yes' responses with Alison – 'Absolutely delighted... Very important step for the professionalization of teaching in higher education... Glad to see acknowledgment of SEDA's pioneering role.'

As the call came to an end, I was struck by two conflicting emotions. This must have shown on my face. 'Well, is it good news or bad?' asked a concerned Kit, our teenage son. Emotion one – 'We've done it!' Emotion two – 'SEDA's teacher accreditation work produces 30 per cent of SEDA's turnover. Now what?'

'Well, it's a long story, Kit.' He sighed and returned to the delights of navigating the narrow boat. I ruminated on the news from the phone call.

The year before, in 1996, a National Commission of Inquiry into Higher Education (the Dearing Committee) had been established. It considered, among other things, the training and accreditation of university teachers, and asked interested organizations to make submissions. When the SEDA Teacher Accreditation Committee and Executive met to consider what SEDA should say in its submission to Dearing, the meetings were vigorous and a whole range of views were expressed.

'Let's push as hard as we can for teacher accreditation to be national policy,' said Chris, one of our particularly enthusiastic members.

'We believe that teaching in higher education should be a professional business and we've shown accreditation *can* work,' said Carole in her encouraging way.

'Look, this is a once-in-a-generation chance to try to make a difference – to get teacher accreditation to be national policy,' enthused Liz.

'They'll never go for teacher accreditation – let's just keep on doing what we're doing,' said Geoff, from the modest self-effacing wing of the committee.

It looked like opinions were poles apart, and the submission date was looming.

Which way will SEDA go in its submission? Why?

PART 2

'Let's just go for it.' This careful and rational analysis won the day at the SEDA Executive meeting. SEDA's written submission and evidence to the Dearing Committee suggested that all university teachers should undertake accredited development for their teaching work. We said that our experience since 1992 had shown that new teaching staff accepted the need for training in teaching, generally welcomed such provision, and valued a transferable national qualification in higher education teaching. We said that universities valued the clear statements of outcomes and underpinning values that the SEDA scheme offered, as well as the freedom to design and run a programme that best met local needs. We suggested that such programmes might normally comprise a post-graduate certificate. And we also suggested, rather cheekily, that this accreditation should be undertaken through the SEDA Teacher Accreditation Scheme.

'Students have the right to be taught well' was the unarguable proposition with which Liz, our chair, and I began our oral evidence to the committee. 'And training and accrediting teachers can make a powerful contribution to this.' One or two other organizations also made broadly similar proposals, and the arguments were clearly persuasive. Dearing recommended, among other things, in words I first heard in the Welsh rain, that 'over the medium term, it should become the normal requirement that all new full-time academic staff with teaching responsibilities are required to achieve at least associate membership of the [Dearing-proposed] Institute for Learning and Teaching in Higher Education, for the successful completion of probation', and that 'It should become the norm for all permanent staff with teaching responsibilities to be trained on accredited programmes.'

Members of the SEDA Teacher Accreditation Committee were delighted that our bright idea had been recommended as national policy. We felt that this vindicated the huge effort that had gone into our scheme – from staff developers, course leaders and course participants as well as senior managers who had backed the scheme. More parochially, but understandably, we were delighted that the Dearing approach of national accreditation of courses, successful completion of which leads to accreditation of individual lecturers, was based on the SEDA Teacher Accreditation Scheme.

But the fear that we had agonized over in committee and that had struck me so forcibly on the boat was now real and immediate – what should SEDA do about its own teacher accreditation work?

What options does SEDA have?
What strategies can SEDA adopt?

PART 3

SEDA had little conventional political power. It was not an agency of government or of the universities. It was an independent membership organization, funded by its few hundred members and by sales of publications and conference places. It was big enough to have a full-time professional administrative team, but it was not used either to the limelight or to the corridors of power. We had to learn, and fast.

Well before Dearing reported, it was clear that he was likely to recommend some form of systematic teacher development and accreditation, but it seemed unlikely that he would make precise recommendations on how accreditation should be implemented. There exists in the UK a tradition of a very technical approach to developing vocational qualifications. One such vocational qualification for higher education teaching had already been developed. Finding no support, it had been laid to rest. We were concerned that such an approach might be tried again. We decided, in a further rush of optimism, to see how much further we could push SEDA's approach to teacher accreditation.

Working closely with the Association of University Teachers (AUT), the trade union that represents staff in the UK's old universities, we established a working party of the main organizations interested in higher education teacher development and accreditation. To chair the group, we invited a widely respected, recently retired Vice-Chancellor, Clive (now Sir Clive) Booth, from Oxford Brookes University, which was renowned for taking the development of teaching very seriously. With a few phone calls we obtained the necessary funding from the UK funding councils – raising money was never so easy, before or since!

Over a few months, the Booth Committee developed a two-stage qualification for part-time and then full-time teachers, with a progression route between them. The proposed qualification was in many ways similar to SEDA's, with simply stated outcomes and a set of underpinning professional values. The committee added a new element – required underpinning knowledge, on topics including student learning and different approaches to teaching. The Booth Committee's proposed scheme fitted well with Dearing's recommendations and was generally very well accepted. (Another complex vocational qualification for higher education teachers was proposed at about this time, but again failed to gain significant support.)

In the meanwhile, the Institute for Learning and Teaching in Higher Education (ILTHE) was established and began work in 1999. After wide consultation, it adopted a framework very similar to that which the Booth Committee had proposed. Once again, SEDA was feeling pleased with both strategy and outcome.

Given a target to recruit a large membership very quickly, the ILTHE established, alongside a process to accredit programmes, a direct entry route for experienced staff through submission of an application. It gave blanket accreditation to all current SEDA-recognized programmes and fellowships, and all graduates of SEDA-recognized courses were accepted as meeting the requirements for direct entry to the ILTHE. By the end of October 2002 over 14,000 staff had successfully applied to join the ILTHE.

In the face of this, SEDA's teacher accreditation work seemed very unlikely to have a long-term future. It was a very different environment, with the ILTHE now a very live reality rather than just a plan. SEDA again faced the question of what it should do about its teacher accreditation work.

Given the huge role and scale of ILTHE, what options does SEDA have for its teacher accreditation?
What effect will this have on SEDA as an organization?

PART 4

'I'm still going to stay with SEDA at least for the time being even after I've got ILTHE accreditation for my programme.' Tony's remark surprised me. Further probing revealed that Tony, like many programme leaders, knew and liked SEDA's approach. The archetypal account of SEDA's programme recognition and review process was that it was 'both challenging and supportive'. It was 'challenging' because SEDA asked many detailed questions about exactly how the programme met SEDA's requirements, and needed a high standard of proof to be satisfied. It was 'supportive' because SEDA appreciated the good ideas in the programme, shared good ideas from other programmes, and had a relatively informal approach on the day. 'Both challenging and supportive' added up to a shared intention to ensure that each programme was as good as it could be, with few preconceptions about the ways in which a programme can be good.

Some programme leaders stayed with SEDA because they liked the SEDA outcomes and values, and indeed had designed their programmes to meet them. They also wanted to be sure that the ILTHE had a secure future before they abandoned SEDA recognition, despite the costs of gaining and retaining recognition/accreditation from both organizations.

The ILTHE, on the other hand, was keen that SEDA cease its teacher accreditation work on an appropriate timescale, and began a process of negotiation with SEDA. It was concerned about possible confusion in the sector, given two similar teacher accreditation schemes in operation. So SEDA staff found themselves in a quandary.

We saw the logic of stopping our teacher accreditation work – as a development association we had developed a good and effective process, and a close variant of this process was now national policy and fast becoming national practice. On the other hand, we were a membership organization, which could only do, or stop doing, things at the behest of our members. And then there was the money.

After much discussion and debate, we decided to go back to our roots, to concentrate again on staff and educational development. This meant:

- confirming and extending the close working relations we had built with our members;
- shifting our focus from anyone interested in teaching and learning and towards staff and educational developers and others interested to innovate in their teaching and support of learning;
- growing the SEDA Fellowship, the established professional qualification for staff and educational developers, into a development process as well as a qualification;
- acknowledging the fast-changing scene around the enhancement of the quality of teaching and learning in higher education.

The last point included new government-funded agencies and initiatives with very large budgets (tens of millions of pounds) for staff and educational development, providing major resources at low or zero cost to users. It also included the changing demands on staff and educational developers, no longer concerned just with training new teaching staff and running development projects, but now contributing, for example, to the writing and implementation of university learning and teaching and human resources strategies, both bringing substantial government funding.

After several iterations and many consultations we got to the idea of a single SEDA professional development framework – we call this SEDA-PDF. The SEDA-PDF describes a process of professional development and learning, and continues the idea of 'recognizing' programmes. It is based heavily on Kolb's learning cycle and has five elements. Those successfully undertaking and completing a SEDA-PDF recognized programme have:

- identified their own professional development goals, directions or priorities;
- made a plan for their initial and/or continuing professional development;
- undertaken appropriate development activities;
- achieved particular specialist outcomes as described for a named award;

- reviewed their development and their practice, and the relations between them.

'Specialist outcomes as described for a named award' needs a little spelling out. Specific named awards (professional qualifications) within SEDA-PDF include 'Supervising Postgraduate Research', 'Supporting Learning' and 'Embedding Learning Technologies'. Each award has a particular set of outcomes as well as the generic development outcomes listed above. For example two specialist outcomes for the Supervising Postgraduate Research named award are the ability (i) to use an appropriate range of methods (and skills) to monitor, examine and assess student progress and attainment, and give feedback on work, and (ii) to supervise production and assessment of the research project (thesis).

In the spirit of SEDA, we don't require that programmes run in exactly this way, only that these processes are clearly visible to and experienced by programme participants. We also retained the use of underpinning values, and additionally adopted Booth and ILTHE's concept of underpinning knowledge. Underpinning and informing the work of those who successfully undertake and complete any SEDA-PDF recognized programme are commitments to:

- an understanding of how people learn;
- scholarship, professionalism and ethical practice;
- working in and developing learning communities;
- working effectively with diversity and promoting inclusivity;
- continued reflection on professional practice;
- the development both of people and of educational processes and systems.

SEDA-PDF embraces both initial and continuing professional development. There are no requirements that a SEDA-PDF programme is at any particular academic level, or of any particular duration, or that it is assessed, or that it brings any particular number of credit points. Explicit attention to the process of development, together with the specified underpinnings, are the core requirements.

SEDA has returned to its roots. How attractive and successful will SEDA-PDF prove to our communities? We don't yet know!

CASE REPORTER'S DISCUSSION

What was it about the approach to accreditation developed by SEDA, and then revised by the Booth Committee, and revised again and implemented by the Institute for Learning and Teaching, that appealed to teachers and staff developers?

From very many conversations with course leaders and course participants at workshops, course validation and review events and assessment boards, I have learnt that people like this approach because they recognize the outcomes as a description of the things they do as teachers. They like the idea that teaching is more than a collection of skills – that it is based on particular values, and underpinned by particular knowledge about learning and teaching as well as about the discipline taught.

Course leaders like the freedom to design their programmes to meet the distinct needs and circumstances of their institution and staff, while holding the assurance of a national standard. The management literature talks of 'loose–tight coupling', of the need to specify some things and let people locally determine other things. 'Tight on outcomes and underpinnings, loose on methods of implementation' seems to have worked well here.

What else have I learnt over these 12 years? For me this is a story about confidence. We had what seemed to us a good idea, teacher accreditation, and we pushed it out into practice to see whether it would float or sink. I'm sure that another year of development of SEDA's initial Teacher Accreditation Scheme, and of subsequent schemes, would have made the schemes better. I am also sure that putting them into practice early, and improving then in light of experience and feedback, made them better much faster.

It is a story about how developers work. Academic developers, I feel, must be principled, proactive opportunists. We must be principled in that we know in what broad directions we want to go – in this case, towards improving teaching and learning and towards professionalizing teaching. We are principled also in that we know broadly what values and beliefs inform our practice – in this case, the belief that students have the right to be taught well, and the belief that staff development and accreditation are good ways to help achieve this as well as the values listed above. We are proactive in that we 'just do' potentially good things, such as developing and launching a teacher accreditation scheme, and later playing a leading role in setting up the Booth Committee. And we are opportunists in that we must be prepared to hitch our wagon to any star that is passing in a broadly appropriate direction – in this case, to the Dearing Committee and then to the ILTHE.

It is also a story about colleagueship and community. Staff development in UK universities used to be a solitary business – a staff development unit might comprise half a person. The scale of development activity has grown enormously. The existence of a strong and self-supporting association of staff and educational developers made some of the developments here possible. At the same time, the activities supported and strengthened the association and its members. I don't want to get too *Lord of the Rings* about this, but a difficult quest and a strong association support each other well.

Acknowledgements

I am enormously grateful to all the many colleagues in SEDA and latterly the ILTHE who have led, undertaken and supported the many and various initiatives described here; to the many programme leaders and staff with whom I have had (often very lively!) debates about the issues and the practices involved in training and accrediting university teachers; to other colleagues across higher education in the other organizations described here for their major contributions to advancing understanding and practice; and to the participants in these programmes who wanted to improve their teaching, and who helped us develop and validate ways to help them do so. This has been a team effort, and will continue to be so, whatever future forms it takes.

Resources

See www.seda.ac.uk

CHAPTER 18

TAKE ONE COUNTRY...

Case reporter: Suki Ekaratne

Issues raised

The issues raised in this case are how to gain acceptance from universities and university staff that staff development is needed for personal, institutional and national development, and then how to bring about this development across a country.

Background

This case takes place in Sri Lanka. The initial problem was the long-standing high level of unemployability among new graduates. This eventually culminated in graduate-led social discontent, resulting in social upheavals and disharmony on a national scale that led to the universities remaining closed for two years. Subsequent analysis identified the need to build greater social accountability by universities, and the need to change teaching practices towards more student-centred methods and the development of employment-linked skills in university students. The University Grants Commission (UGC) thereafter made it mandatory for all newly recruited junior academic staff to follow a staff development course on new teaching and assessment methods.

As no such course was then available in Sri Lanka to meet this requirement, the UGC also recommended the establishment of staff development centres (SDCs) to run such courses. Colombo University established the first such centre, with the case reporter, who was trained as an aquatic ecologist, as its first director.

PART 1

Day One. An office, an assistant, and a brief that looked larger and less possible every minute I thought about it. Why hadn't I stuck to aquatic biology, to coral?

If in doubt, I learnt a long time ago, make a list. A list may not solve the problem, but it will certainly clarify it. Here is the list of questions I wrote:

- What should we do to identify and then meet the staff development and training needs?
- How far can we extend our services in the light of the limited funding and staffing?
- How can we locate more resources?
- How can I ensure the quality of the training activities?

An answer to this generated a further question:

- How can I benchmark our work against international practice and standards?

The questions began to sharpen, always a good sign:

- How can I generate funds to identify overseas practice and standards, and then regularly to bring in the necessary resource people from overseas?

OK, these were a useful set of questions about needs analysis and standards and resources. But, I realized, answers to these questions would not solve all my problems. For example:

- How can we win the support and confidence of the different categories of our home university's staff?
- How can we induce in particular the senior staff to become retrained?
- How can I build a critical mass of changed staff in order to sustain changed practices?
- What would happen if I was unable to succeed in changing staff attitudes and practices, and what change strategies should I then adopt?

I know that training programmes can quickly become stale and lose relevance. So:

- How often would I need to review training needs and methods and change them to accommodate changing circumstances?

The more I thought about what I was trying to do, the more I realized that resources and workshops and outside experts alone would not do it all. Change needs to be embedded. I moved on to asking:

- How can I influence policy?

I then saw that this was a bigger question than I had first realized:

- How can I influence policy at the level of my home university, of all universities in the country and at national level?

Finally I saw that, whatever the answers to these questions, I also had to address some very local questions if the venture was to have any chance of success:

- How will I empower the only support staff member available to me to take on responsibility for functions far above her official duties?
- And how, and to what extent, should I train myself to take on these new functions?

I was a senior professorial-level academic. I had experience as a recognized researcher in my academic discipline – aquatic biology – and some credibility as a change agent. I had extensive experience in student counselling and support, but I had no formal training in staff development. Before the establishment of the SDC, the vice-chancellor of the university, who was well aware of the lack of staff development practices and expertise in the country, had earmarked a three-month period of overseas exposure and training for me as the centre's first director. The vice-chancellor had also requested the Commonwealth Fund for Technical Cooperation in the UK to fund a one-year consultancy assignment to bring in an experienced overseas staff developer to work with me.

This was a good start, but problems remained. The selected consultant, Stephen, had great staff development expertise, but he had no experience in working within the limited resources available in a developing country. On the positive side, however, we were housed within the Vice-Chancellery and we had the unstinting support and goodwill of the vice-chancellor.

How should the director begin his task?
What are the best ways to utilize an overseas consultant?
Will a study tour be beneficial? How?

PART 2

Applying my scientific training and trying to ignore my continued fluttering of concern, I analysed the prevailing conditions, identified the lack of practices or of a resource base of staff trainers within the country, then took various steps to try to improve the situation, identifying issues and adapting practices from other countries to suit local situations as we went along.

To carry out the intended work effectively, I needed to obtain, maintain and use the active support and cooperation of a wide cross-section of the university community, ranging from the visiting consultant, vice-chancellor, deans, heads of department, administrative staff, junior and senior lecturers, clerical and junior support staff; and of course my clerical assistant, the whole support staff of the SDC!

'I'm really not sure that the staff development methods I use in the UK, the sort of teaching methods I advocate there, will go down very well here.' I understood Stephen's concern. To be honest, I wasn't sure either. I knew from my reading and conversations that UK higher education was making more use of interactive teaching and learning methods, with more emphasis on students being active in class. 'Let's take it slowly,' I suggested. And this is how we worked – gently introducing participant activity into the staff development workshops, seeing how staff reacted to it, and then exploring with them how they might use such approaches, or variants of them, in their own teaching.

Stephen's initial anxiety quickly reduced. I made the working environment an open and flexible one, as well as seeing that his domestic needs were satisfied. And, as Stephen put it as we talked after one workshop, 'Staff developers have to be adaptable people! Working in a new country is rather like working in a new discipline, only much more so.'

Stephen wasn't the only one who was concerned; I also needed to reduce the anxiety of the university staff towards the newly established SDC and to our work. Beyond that, I needed to raise their curiosity with regard to what this new centre was setting out to do, and indeed was capable of doing.

We accomplished this in several ways. The most important was that participants in the workshops went back to their departments and reported that the experience, though unusual, was not outrageous or silly and that, yes, some of the ideas worked well and led to good student learning once students had become used to them. Introducing Stephen to the university officials such as the deans made it possible to establish contact and mutual respect. The anxieties of the deans with regard to the activities of the centre were allayed, and their confidence in the SDC was developed, by convening a meeting of the deans and by incorporating their identified staff training needs in the training agenda of the SDC.

I decided not to proceed on the planned three-month overseas training visit, but to attempt on-the-job self-training. I allowed the possibility of some overseas exposure visits after the centre and its activities had become established.

We developed a suite of programmes. A training course for junior staff was drawn up by the consultant, with advice from me, and approval and accreditation for the course was obtained from the university Senate and from the

UGC. The topics that the deans had identified were included as training workshops – these generated much interest and attendance. Further workshops were designed on topics that Stephen and I thought were appropriate. We published a regular newsletter and circulated it to all staff members in the home university, and to deans and vice-chancellors of the other universities in the country. Through this staff were informed of training workshops and courses, and were invited to attend these activities.

Because the junior staff course was the only course being offered nationally to meet the mandatory requirement for junior academics, it attracted many more applicants than we could teach in a single batch. Rather than restrict numbers to a single cohort and turn away many applicants, and despite the large workload involved, we decided to run the course in two parallel cohorts.

The dedicated commitment of the support staff of the SDC, as well as that of the administrative staff in the university, was obtained by conducting the work in an open and non-hierarchical manner. The respect of university staff, the active support of the vice-chancellor and the strategic location of the centre all helped considerably in obtaining the support of both academic and administrative staff. Often, we would invite the vice-chancellor for workshops and he would himself start off the training workshops with a few words of introduction and support. This gave the activities of the centre considerable credibility and clout. We used feedback questionnaires continuously, to assess the acceptability of our workshops and to obtain information on other workshop topics that were desired by staff. We strove to offer training workshops in identified areas, thereby attracting a large number of interested staff to our workshops.

And we knew that the programme was working. We were delighted to hear, in later workshops, such a statement from a lecturer as, 'I asked students to work in small groups to prepare and give presentations on particular topics to the rest of the class. Many of them weren't used to speaking in public, and some were very nervous, but they worked hard on their preparations and the other students were very appreciative.' As both the junior and senior staff began to introduce the new and interactive methods to their own teaching, the credibility and acceptability of the centre began to grow.

The centre was helped considerably by the juniors' course being accredited by the Staff and Educational Development Association of the United Kingdom (SEDA). Further help was given by the appointment of Elizabeth, an experienced British staff developer, as the external examiner for the course, and by her visits to the centre to examine the material produced in the course and to offer us formative feedback.

Since feedback questionnaires revealed that senior staff would benefit from a similar course, in addition to the bespoke workshops, we designed and delivered a course to senior staff. Through our vice-chancellor, the Committee of Vice-Chancellors and Directors (CVCD) invited our consultant Stephen to deliver a talk on staff development at one of their monthly meetings. To gain support from another important sector of the university community, the deans and heads of department, their training needs were addressed by designing and conducting a training programme of monthly workshops that was entitled a 'Management Development Programme'.

As the end of our first year of activities approached and Stephen's period of service as overseas consultant was nearing its end, we managed to generate overseas funding for the centre. These funds were used to extend his consultancy by another few months and when he completed his extended term, available funding was used to bring in other overseas resource persons to conduct training workshops for academic staff. This maintained the input of quality staff to the training workshops programme. I ensured the quality of all resource persons, internal and external, by bringing in only persons that I had seen delivering quality workshop sessions either locally or at overseas meetings. A regular programme of excellent workshops was put in place to service training needs of staff from both home and all national universities.

I believed it was very important to identify excellent-quality overseas consultants as well as to select workshop topics to cater to local needs. The use of e-mail was vital in negotiating this. For these overseas consultants, it was necessary to arrange good-quality accommodation and working facilities as well as timely production of hand-out material. This was made possible by planning well ahead so that the necessary administrative approvals by the various committees were obtained in time. Elizabeth, our external examiner, also conducted workshops when she visited the centre for examination work.

As the SDC became known nationally among the universities, and as word spread of the activities of the centre, I was invited by the UGC to address workshops on how the activities of the centre were organized and carried out, so that the SDC could help model staff development activities for other universities. The private sector, which is the main employment sector in the country, invited me to join the Human Resources Committee of their association, the Ceylon Chamber of Commerce. Through this committee, I established a discussion forum between the private sector and junior university academics, which became known as the Chamber Academia Round Table (CART). As the topics of discussion at CART progressed and became known, senior academics including vice-chancellors began to attend its monthly sessions. Thus, through the Ceylon Chamber of Commerce, and in particular through working together in CART, both the UGC and national-level private sector companies began to value more highly training and the meeting of employability needs.

With Stephen leaving and the increase in the volume of staff development work that I was continuously called upon to deliver, it soon became clear that staff developers needed to be trained from among university staff if this growing interest was to be sustained. I then organized a five-day residential 'Training the Trainers' workshop for 25 interested senior staff from all the national universities, with a highly respected and highly committed overseas staff trainer-developer as the resource person. This was carried out annually so that individual universities could plan out, as well as commence, conducting staff development and training activities in their own universities, even on a small scale. For any training needs that they were unable to deliver, these universities would send staff to the SDC training activities that we conducted. Also, a selection of quality staff were sent to overseas staff development workshops to gain knowledge and experience in teaching-related methodology and in research presentations.

As other universities established their own staff development centres, the directors of these centres consulted our centre for guidance. They then began to replicate our practices. Some also began to establish their own courses for junior staff.

With staff development work expanding, the need to establish formal nation-wide structures was perceived. The UGC established a Standing Committee for Staff Development. This forum provided for monthly meetings of all directors of staff development units from all the national universities, chaired by the UGC chair. At higher forums also, such as at meetings of the Committee of Vice-Chancellors and Directors (CVCD), staff development initiatives were discussed. The CVCD invited me to draft a document for adoption for the 'professionalization' of university academics. The university system did not have a structure for recognizing the career path for staff developers as an academic discipline – because staff development had not hitherto been recognized as a discipline. I brought this to the attention of the Standing Committee, and was invited by the Committee to formulate and submit a document whereby such recognition would be made possible.

What do you think of the conclusions that were reached and the ideas adopted for training of junior and senior staff?
What would you have done differently?
What lessons can you draw from this case for your own staff training practices?

CASE REPORTER'S DISCUSSION

This was a long process. What have I learnt from it?

It was important to start by recognizing a national need, and then finding a possible process – in this case, staff development towards more student-centred and employment-related learning. Simply starting with some general wish to improve learning and teaching would have been much less effective. It was also important to get the balance right between planning the process and adapting to changed needs and new circumstances and possibilities, seeking out such changes rather than being surprised by them.

Varied support, at many levels, in the university and then in the country was vital, as was the quantity of support – forming a critical mass of staff and managers in favour of change; having formed this critical mass, marshalling it to support change; and continuing to maintain, enhance and develop this critical mass. Also vital was reducing anxiety about change in stakeholders and potential stakeholders, through wide consultation before we started and then by keeping academics informed and involved throughout the development process.

I put a lot of effort into applying and replicating good practice from the university, the country and other countries, benchmarking against international standards. I found financial resources and used them to maintain both momentum and quality.

To ensure the longer-term health and growth of university staff development in Sri Lanka I wrote and talked about the centre and its activities so that others could adopt or adapt our ideas and practices; I worked with the corporate sector nationally, to ensure relevance of and gain support for the work; and I managed to get a national change agency established, recognized, supported and sustained.

But while I took a leadership role in all of this, it was made possible by the generous involvement and support of many people. That's how staff development works.

SECTION 5

BECOMING A DEVELOPER

CHAPTER 19

Ways to make things better – one, two, three!

Case reporter: Alison Holmes

Issue raised

The issue raised in this case is career progression for lecturers who are bored with their subject area but remain fascinated by teaching and learning.

Background

This case occurs mainly in the northeast of England. A female lecturer in surveying at a large polytechnic is now in the middle of her career, and has many years' experience as both a professional surveyor and more recently a lecturer.

PART 1

'How had it come to this?' I wondered as I dragged myself to the car park on a rainy Thursday afternoon. How could I be so disenchanted with my lot?

I remember well my introduction to teaching in a polytechnic. It was two weeks before start of term, in my brand new job as a lecturer in surveying. 'Off you go!' said the head of department as he handed me the syllabus and timetable. That was it, that and an induction course for new lecturers that the polytechnic ran. But I only completed the first session of this induction course, on presentation skills, then I went on maternity leave. No one seemed to mind; teaching just didn't seem to matter. Some seven years later, 'having teaching experience' gained me a job at another polytechnic, and exemption from the new lecturers' course there. There was no need to demonstrate anything about the content or quality of my teaching.

But things did begin to change as far as teaching was concerned. Within three years, all new lecturers were required to do the newly developed PG Certificate in University Teaching and Learning (PGCUTL). I didn't have to do it because I was by this time considered experienced! As an exam paper might have asked, 'Experienced equals competent. Discuss.'

The wider world of higher education was changing also. It was soon to be our turn to be subject to the UK Quality Assurance Agency's subject review. This was an intensive process that probed every aspect of the operation of a department and its courses, and published scores and a detailed commentary. It was, to put it mildly, a stressful and demanding affair. In preparation for the onslaught, a cut-down version of the PGCUTL was devised to be delivered over six days for members of the department who had never undergone any kind of teacher training. The course was formally known as 'Building on Experience', less formally as 'Teaching for Old Wrinklies'.

On the first run through, we were 12 participants with over 300 years of teaching experience between us! The six-day course validated a lot of the practices we had developed through instinct and trial and error, boosted our confidence, and, for me at least, also boosted feelings of credibility as a teacher. We all learnt new things and I loved it. Even the most sceptical acknowledged its benefits.

Bolstered by this confidence, and by my experience and interest in teaching, I became the chair of the Departmental Teaching and Learning Committee shortly after this. I worked with other teaching and learning enthusiasts in the department. We ran staff development sessions, created a teaching resources centre and engaged with the central educational development service's 'Alternative Learning Week' where we showcased innovative practice. These were the best bits of my working week. I was able to visibly and explicitly work on learning and teaching instead of pretending to do research into surveying, which no longer appealed. It was an exciting time and my level of work satisfaction was high.

'Would you like to go through a pilot version of the UK Staff and Educational Development Association (SEDA) 'Accredited Teacher' scheme?' asked David one morning at breakfast during the annual conference. 'It will be an opportunity to get your teaching experience formally recognized, and build on the enthusiasm interest in teaching and learning opportunity which running the committee has fuelled.' I jumped at the chance. I had been teaching for years, but had no piece of paper to evidence my teaching ability.

SEDA was exploring ways of giving accreditation to experienced staff. I was to be part of the pilot to be run by the Educational Development Service at the university. I had to read those fascinating books in the Learning Resources Centre so that I could reference the kind of techniques I was using and demonstrate how I knew they were appropriate. I was required to reflect on my activities and to show how I had improved my teaching practice. I really enjoyed the support sessions, having heated discussions about how students learn, why some techniques work and others don't, and observing videos of my own and others' teaching. My biggest regret about working for this accreditation was that there was never enough time to do all the reading that I wanted to, and I ended up often just doing the minimum to get through. Wouldn't it be great to have time to read these books properly? I could see that they held lots of good ideas, and even some answers to the challenges of the changing student population.

September came round again. I returned to work and started preparing for next year's teaching, wondering how I could improve the courses I delivered. I had moved on a long way from the early days of simply reading out my notes. I now engaged in interactive lectures; created workbooks for the students to encourage independent learning; and had designed and written a computer-aided learning package with a colleague. As I reflected on the ways I delivered my modules and wondered how I could reinvent my wheel yet again, I realized that my greatest pleasure in teaching came when I was able to help students achieve their best, whether they were top or bottom of the class. It was the people, not the content of the courses, that had become the centre of my life. Seeing a student who had developed slowly over the years come back six months after graduation as a confident, competent trainee surveyor made the job worthwhile.

But I was getting increasingly bored with my subject. Surveying the still-wrapped semester's worth of weekly trade magazines that I knew I should read to keep me up to date with my subject, my heart sank. 'Do you still enjoy reading the *Estates Gazette*?' I asked Anne as we collected our mail from the pigeonholes. 'Oh yes,' she said. 'I just love reading about investment and valuation and passing the information onto my students.' That did it for me. How could I teach students when I no longer had enthusiasm for my subject?

What do you think is the main problem here?
What options could Alison consider?

PART 2

'You see, John,' I said to my line manager at my next annual appraisal, 'I feel stuck in a rut – just going round the same cycle year after year in predictable monotony. It's actually the people who interest me, not teaching about the property and facilities management. You know I enjoyed doing the SEDA accreditation. But I found it really frustrating not having the time to read the literature.' His response surprised me. 'Have you seen that advertisement on the board for someone to work in the new Quality Enhancement Unit (QEU)?'

I hadn't, but when I looked, the closing date was past. Nevertheless, I talked to the head of the QEU, who said, 'We haven't appointed because there weren't enough applicants. We are reconstructing the post. It will be readvertised at the end of the month.' I duly spent two days at the end of the month, when I should have been packing for my summer holidays, writing a job application, and posted it as we drove south for the ferry to France.

The holiday was relaxing, and on my return I was interviewed and then offered the job. I accepted with delight. 'Brilliant!' I thought. 'No more property, no more marking, no more fighting about rooms and timetables.' Then other thoughts began to appear, like much less contact (in fact almost none) with the students, and where would the job satisfaction come from? But, the opportunity for change was there, and I took it without too much further navel-gazing.

QEU was a great place to work. We, a team of two academics and two support staff, invented our jobs as we went along, and tried to lead by example, with a 'can do' mentality. We always tried to say 'yes' and then think of a way of achieving what we had promised to deliver afterwards! Our achievements were many and varied – a wide-ranging programme of staff development; annual course leaders' conferences; and national Institutional Facilitator conferences. We prepared departments for Quality Assurance Agency (QAA) subject review and helped them achieve excellent scores; devised and supported implementation of new rules and regulations about assessment; ran quality audits of learning resources, assessment, student support, guidance and student feedback; and supported faculty quality committee monitoring, to name but a few. Quality enhancement was certainly the name of our game, but we also undertook quality assurance activities, always from an enhancement perspective.

The move to the Quality Enhancement Unit made me more aware of the whole business of quality assurance of courses and policy decision making related to teaching and learning. As a teacher, I used to think that all this was imposed on us front-line workers by people who had no knowledge of teaching. I had now joined that central machinery. We worked very hard to apply many of the directives coming from outside the university in a sympathetic way that attempted to follow the ethos of the university and to provide the best for our students and staff alike. Of course it wasn't always received that way by the academics! I came to see what the purpose of all those quality assurance forms was, and how they could be used to improve the practice right across the university. My role had shifted, but my focus was the same – improving student learning.

'I just can't face this tonight,' I thought as I stared at the ring binder in my briefcase. Helping people to explore their own practice and decide what they really want to create for their students was a fascinating experience, and widened my knowledge about teaching and learning greatly. The most visible part of our work, the preparation of departments for subject review, gave us the handle for a lot of staff development workshops and seminars, where staff started to think about learning outcomes and assessment criteria. However, the thought of reading yet another self-assessment document, like the one in the ring binder in my briefcase, was like looking at the pile of shrink-wrapped *Estates Gazettes* – a key part of my job had lost its intrinsic attraction. The increasing emphasis on rules and regulations, and making sure everyone was complying with the QAA Code of Practice, had begun to make me like a police officer – which is not really in my nature.

I had found a way to broaden my experience while in the QEU. It had taken me four years to become a qualified surveyor, allowed to sign my own reports, and it had taken me four minutes to be given the syllabus and the timetable before I was inflicted on unsuspecting students. It had always seemed wrong to me that, just because I was a qualified surveyor, it was assumed that I had the ability and underpinning knowledge to teach. So when the newly established Institute for Learning and Teaching in Higher Education (ILTHE) was looking to appoint accreditors, to assess individual applications for entry and to accredit courses for new lecturers, I applied, and was accepted. This was my opportunity to help raise the profile of teaching and the public perception of the quality of lecturing across the country, and further my knowledge and understanding of teaching through the discussions that accreditors have as they assess applications for membership, and visit universities to accredit postgraduate certificate courses for new lecturers.

'Have you seen the ad?' asked Rosie, a long-time friend and informal mentor. 'It's right up your alley. A job in the National Coordination Team would just suit you and your experience.'

I rang the team director and asked her how she would characterize the job. Without a hesitation she said 'educational development'. I applied, again at the holiday season, was accepted and started working for the Higher Education Funding Council for England's (HEFCE) National Coordination Team (NCT) for the Teaching Quality Enhancement Fund (TQEF). My main role was to help and support teams get good value for the £250,000 (or thereabouts) they had won from the HEFCE to disseminate good practice in some aspect of teaching and learning.

The position widened my vision, this time from a single university to the whole sector. I now supported almost 20 projects, visited many different universities, and engaged with staff at all levels from vice-chancellor down. Being seen as the HEFCE representative had plus sides (they listen to you) and negative ones (they think you are a police officer!). But I could observe and help in one situation, and take that information and transfer it to another university or project team. This is similar to a role I played in the QEU – a conduit for sharing practices around the university. Now I was doing it around the country.

Over time, however, I began to really miss the students, and wondered if I had just become a paper shuffler who really had no impact on students' lives.

One day, as I travelled home by train, I was busy writing up a project visit report. The man beside me could see from my paperwork that I worked with universities, and asked me where we might have met before. Eventually, we realized that I had given a presentation at a two-day event on assessment that he had attended earlier in the year. In the conversation that followed, I expressed my concern about no longer having any real impact on students. His response remains with me, and strengthens my resolve. 'If you can help 40 lecturers each improve their practice so that each of their 200 students per annum benefit, then you are doing a more worthwhile job.' Thank you!

CASE REPORTER'S DISCUSSION

Would I have done better to keep one foot in the active teaching camp? I wonder. At the time, I didn't feel it was an option, but I have to say that I did not explore it thoroughly. I felt very disillusioned with teaching at the time, because of the increasing pressures I saw being placed on rank and file lecturers.

Since the TQEF has been supporting learning and teaching strategies in institutions, there are many universities where 'learning and teaching coordinators' (or some other similar title) have been appointed. Often these posts are fractional, the post holder spending the rest of his or her time teaching, or for a fixed term. They are designed to spearhead activities to improve the quality of teaching and learning in the faculty or institution. That would certainly have been of interest to me had there been such an opportunity at the time I joined the QEU, as I really did feel I was burning my bridges by moving out of lecturing altogether. Fortunately for me the move into educational development has been such fun, and so rewarding, that I have no regrets – well, only a very few.

As to my credibility as a developer, where does it come from? I think I have credibility because I have many years of teaching experience; because I have been engaged in many of the quality processes that influence the development of learning and teaching; and because I have a practical approach to getting the job done. Keeping the teaching credibility is possibly the hardest, as you have to remain in touch with the environment of the regular teachers. It is easy to become unrealistic in what you say to lecturers. You forget the grind of lecture preparation, the constant stream of students at the door and the juggling of all the demands for research, administration and teaching.

In addition to keeping my credibility with my teaching colleagues, I have to develop and maintain my credibility with my educational development peers. That means feeding back into the community in a rigorous and scholarly way the learning I am getting from my privileged role as national coordinator.

Once again thanks to SEDA, I am working towards the qualification that gives me formal recognition for the job I do. The SEDA Fellowship Award is made to applicants who can demonstrate that they have achieved the desired objectives and embrace the values of SEDA, and continue to do so. This will give me my external credibility. The rest will come from the way I engage with my projects and with those I encounter more widely in the community.

What of the future? I think my time as a national coordinator may have spoilt me for going back into a single institution – I feel that the wider arena is so much more exciting, and offers the opportunity for really having an impact on the teaching and learning community. The champions and developers of teaching and learning are beginning to have a real impact, but there is still a long way for us to go. But as this book goes to press, I have just accepted the job of Quality Enhancement Manager at Derby University. I find that I am looking forward to using there what I have learned in a national role over the last two years. My role and methods have shifted again, but again my focus remains the same – improving student learning. I hope the man on the train would agree that I am still doing something useful.

CONCLUSION: INSIGHTS FROM THE CASE STUDIES

Change, enthusiasm, struggle, variety – these are some of the words that spring to mind and leap from the pages of the case studies in this book. The range of what staff and educational developers attempt is huge, from individual consultation through to changing the culture in faculties and institutions, and even developing national systems. There is no clear limit to what developers choose to do or are expected to tackle, nor to what they volunteer to tackle. The people undertaking the tasks, the staff and educational developers, have a variety of roles and positions, from being a lone ranger in a new unit through to being part of a government-supported national team. There is no fixed route to becoming a staff and educational developer, nor an acknowledged professional qualification or required experience for entry. More than anything, staff and educational developers are, as Baume concluded in Chapter 17, 'Far too successful', 'principled proactive opportunists'. The cases in this book give abundant examples.

Tackling key issues

To be useful to an organization, staff and educational development must tackle key issues, which are many and varied. The issues may result from institutional decisions, such as to reposition the university or improve the research output, from outside pressures such as government policy, the quality agenda, or from opportunities arising, such as external funding becoming available. We find cases on assessment (Chapter 5, 'And the right answer is...'), on improving retention (Chapter 13, 'Mission impossible?'), on introducing online learning (Chapters 8, 'Walking a tightrope', and 9, 'By accident or...?'), on teachers developing as researchers (Chapter 4, 'Are teachers really researchers?'), on developing academic writing skills (Chapter 2, 'Professional development in retreat'), on recognizing and rewarding good teaching (Chapter 12, 'The seven steps'), and on ensuring students are employable (Chapters 10, 'I will survive', and 11, 'Better together').

Tools of the trade

The cases in this book give a taste of the number and variety of methods that staff and educational developers use. There are examples of working with individuals to improve their practice through the traditional one on one consultation (Chapter 1, 'Yes, but can you prove it?'), of mentoring (Chapter 7, 'Making a difference') and of working directly with small groups of teachers in workshops (Chapters 2, 'Professional development in retreat', and 5, 'And the right answer is...'). These are the traditional tools of staff and educational development. They continue to be effective, give satisfaction to the developers and be useful for their clients.

Developers do not have particular or fixed methodologies that they use – rather they choose an approach that they deem will be effective in the particular situation. This leads to an eclectic and extensive repertoire. Chapters 4, 'Are teachers really researchers?', and 10, 'I will survive', describe the use of action learning. Retreat as a technique gets good results in Chapters 2, 'Professional development in retreat', and 3, 'Mapping the way'. Bringing in the right external consultants can have distinct advantages as Chapters 5, 'And the right answer is...', 14, 'Standing out in a big crowd', and 18, 'Take one country...', demonstrate. It's important for developers to become part of the fabric of an institution and to have powerful decision makers on side, as is evidenced in Chapters 15, 'Too much too soon?', and 18, 'Take one country...'. Using working groups to produce a consensual approach that will get acceptance is time-consuming but effective (Chapter 12, 'The seven steps'). The traditional academic approach of building on published research and on others' experience is used in development work (Chapters 11, 'Better together', and 13, 'Mission impossible?'), though not always with predictable results. And of course there is always 'slowly does it' (Chapter 6, 'The proof of the pudding...') and serendipity (Chapter 9, 'By accident or...?').

Most cases demonstrate that having only one technique or approach to the problem is not sufficient. Finding the solution to difficulties and dilemmas often means using multiple methods and being willing to change approaches. It is seldom possible in staff and educational development to use a 'one size fits all' or 'this is the answer' approach to the task in hand. What works in one situation or institution may not work in another. Staff and educational developers need to be able to analyse the situation in hand, choose and try a methodology, reflect on its effectiveness, and if necessary change. Developers need to be multi-pronged and flexible, and work on many levels at once.

Widening the focus

One of the surprises of putting this book together has been the very wide focus for staff and educational development activities, together with the immensity of the tasks facing the developers. Some case reporters found themselves starting up a unit from scratch, which can be hard, frustrating and lonely work, especially in traditional institutions (Chapters 15, 'Too much too soon?', 16, 'We're not laughing now', and 18, 'Take one country...'). Setting up a new unit requires working at all levels of the institution, and most importantly, gaining credibility with the constituency, both clients and sponsors.

In the UK in recent years, government-funded initiatives and requirements have changed the face and practice of staff and educational development, brought new people into the field and provided career progression for developers. Many of the cases reflect these changes, as they describe working at the level of system and organization development; of implementing major curriculum changes; and of taking advantage of external funding. Chapters 11, 'Better together', 12, 'The seven steps', 14, 'Standing out in a big crowd', and 19, 'Ways to make things better – one, two, three!', are examples.

Developers can find themselves in the position of having to support and develop institutional initiatives that are unpopular with teaching staff and with which they themselves may not agree. This requires skill in turning the situation around, in working with staff who may be feeling negative, and in mining the situation for the best advantages to staff and students (Chapter 8, 'Walking a tightrope'). Often hard decisions like excluding someone have to be taken along the way (Chapter 10, 'I will survive').

Developers face big tasks in these kinds of projects. They are not only or just working with individuals or small groups to change their practice. They are effectively trying to change the culture of an institution that may not necessarily want to change. External funding can provide opportunities for development, but requires specific focus and responsibility for outcomes. Supporting big tasks means translating the generic 'improving teaching and learning' into such things as a capability-based curriculum (Chapter 10, 'I will survive'), making a university distinctive through building a learning community (Chapter 14, 'Standing out in a big crowd'), and realizing measurable improvements in student performance (Chapter 13, 'Mission impossible?').

Staff and educational developers take on the role of facilitating organizational change. While the impetus for the project may come from 'on high' in the institution or through government-funded initiatives, developers are careful to keep their primary aim of improving student learning as the ultimate outcome. The capacity to seize opportunities that are presented, in whatever guise, and yet remain true to staff and educational development principles is the key to much of their success. Chapters 6, 'The proof of the pudding...', 8, 'Walking a tightrope', and 17, 'Far too successful', display this graphically. These case reporters are experienced operators, yet they find themselves in situations that require strategy, cunning, perseverance, skill, guile and luck as well as adherence to basic principles and values in order to be successful. Trying to change institutional culture and approaches is a big task. It is very different from working with individuals or small groups of teachers who want to change and improve their practice. Yet it may now be the essential nature of staff and educational development.

Working at the national level

Staff and educational developers also work across institutions at national level, often in a tight timeframe that makes their task even more demanding. The skills involved are similar to those required for local initiatives, but made complex by the scale of the project. Getting a national scheme of staff development for university teachers in a developing country up and running from scratch, with very few resources and as a part-time appointment, was the daunting task faced by the case reporter in Chapter 18, 'Take one country...'. As the case demonstrates, he was successful. This is a dramatic example of working at the national level, starting from scratch, embedding staff development in all universities in the country and developing a nationally accredited training course for university teachers. The case also highlights some of the difficulties and advantages of working in a developing country.

The vital ingredient: cooperation

The cases in the book cover many situations and countries, yet through them all shines the need for and importance of cooperation. Without cooperation, staff and educational development activities cannot succeed. Getting cooperation can be vital to the success of the method (Chapters 5, 'And the right answer is...', and 13, 'Mission impossible?'), but is not always easy to obtain (Chapters 3, 'Mapping the way', 6, 'The proof of the pudding...', 10, 'I will survive', and 11, 'Better together'). It is possible to cooperate with management in its focus on change and accountability, and still produce good development results (Chapters 8, 'Walking a tightrope', and 12, 'The seven steps'). Cooperation between developers leads to stronger projects (Chapters 16, 'We're not laughing now', and 18, 'Take one country...'). Working together as a professional association and with other interested parties achieves far better outcomes than could be obtained singly (Chapter 17, 'Far too successful').

Good staff and educational development uses cooperation to produce better outcomes.

The professionalization of staff and educational development

The final insight from the cases is around the professionalization of staff and educational development. Can staff and educational development be a profession if there is no agreed body of theory, little proof of efficacy, no qualification or clear process for entry, no career path, and no self-regulation and control? Possibly strictly not, but evidence from the book suggests that the time is not far away.

People come into staff and educational development and move through it in various incarnations (Chapter 19, 'Ways to make things better – one, two, three!'). They reinvent its practice to suit the situation (Chapters 8, 'Walking a tightrope', and 16, 'We're not laughing now'). Note though that much of staff and educational development is carried out by people who are not classified as developers and who get little acknowledgement or support in their efforts (Chapters 3, 'Mapping the way', 6, 'The proof of the pudding...', and 7, 'Making a difference').

Staff and educational development practitioners are beginning to establish processes that will lead to the professionalization of the area, especially in the United Kingdom. By seizing the moment and following their beliefs, the Staff and Educational Development Association (SEDA) had a strong influence on the climate, standards and regulations surrounding the training of university teachers implemented by the government-established Institute for Learning and Teaching in Higher Education (Chapter 17, 'Far too successful'). It also developed a fellowship scheme for staff and educational developers.

The practice of staff and educational development reminds us of Tennyson's *Ulysses* who said:

> I am a part of all that I have met
> Yet all experience is an arch wherethrough
> Gleams that untravelled world, whose margin fades
> For ever and for ever when I move.

New excitements, new challenges and new horizons await. Staff and educational development has changed dramatically. It is more sophisticated and complex; outcomes are sometimes less direct and still difficult to measure. Sponsors have more resources, are more demanding and expect projects to be transferable. Staff and educational developers can rise to the practical challenges, as the cases in this book demonstrate. They need also to find ways of gauging the effectiveness of their efforts, developing the theory of their practice and supporting the emergence of their profession.

FURTHER READING

Books and journal articles

Aylett, R and Gregory, K (eds) (1996) *Evaluating Teacher Quality in Higher Education*, Falmer Press, London

Baume, C, Martin, P and Yorke, M (eds) (2002) *Managing Educational Development Projects*, Kogan Page, London

Baume, D (1995) Staff development for open and flexible learning, in *Flexible Learning Strategies in Higher and Further Education*, ed D Thomas, Cassell, London

Baume, D and Baume, C (1996) A national scheme to develop and accredit university teachers, *International Journal for Academic Development*, **1** (2), pp 51–58.

Baume, D and Kahn, P (eds) (2003) *Enhancing Staff and Educational Development*, Kogan Page, London

Beaty, L (1998) The professional development of teachers in higher education: structures, methods and responsibilities, *Innovations in Education and Training International*, **35** (2), pp 99–107

Becher, T and Trowler, P (2001) *Academic Tribes and Territories: Intellectual enquiry and the culture of disciplines*, 2nd edn, Society for Research into Higher Education (SRHE) and Open University Press, Buckingham

Beerens, D R (2000) *Evaluating Teachers for Professional Growth: Creating a culture of motivation and learning*, Corwin Press, CA

Bess, J L (ed) (1997) *Teaching Well and Liking It: Motivating faculty to teach effectively*, Johns Hopkins University Press, London

Biggs, J (1999) *Teaching for Quality Learning at University*, SRHE and Open University Press, Buckingham

Bolton, A (2000) *Managing the Academic Unit*, Open University Press, Buckingham

Bowden, J and Marton, F (1998) *The University of Learning: Beyond quality and competence in higher education*, Kogan Page, London

Brew, A (1995) *Directions in Staff Development*, SRHE and Open University Press, Buckingham

Brew, A and Boud, D (1996) Preparing for new academic roles: an holistic approach to development, *International Journal for Academic Development*, **1** (2), pp 17–25

Brookfield, S (1995) *Becoming a Critically Reflective Teacher*, Jossey-Bass, San Francisco

Carrotte, P (1999) Turning academics into teachers, S Roland *et al*, *Teaching in Higher Education*, **4** (3), pp 411–13

Cowan, J (1998) *On Becoming an Innovative University Teacher: Reflection in action*, SRHE and Open University Press, Buckingham

Day, K, Grant, R and Hounsell, D (1998) *Reviewing Your Teaching*, Centre for Teaching Learning and Assessment, University of Edinburgh, Edinburgh

DeZure, D (ed) (2002) *Learning From Change: Landmarks in teaching and learning in higher education from Change Magazine, 1969–1999*, Stylus Publishing in association with AAHE, Sterling, VA

Edwards, H, Higgs, J and Everingham, F (1999) Developing as health professional educators, in *Educating Beginning Practitioners: Challenges for health professional education*, ed J Higgs and H Edwards, pp 256–62, Butterworth Heinemann, Oxford

Elton, L (1998) Dimensions of excellence in university teaching, *International Journal for Academic Development*, **3** (1), pp 3–11

Gosling, D (2001) Educational development units in the UK – what are they doing five years on? *International Journal for Academic Development*, **6** (1), pp 74–90

Grant, B and Knowles, S (2000) Flights of imagination: academic women be(com)ing writers, *International Journal for Academic Development*, **5** (1), pp 6–19

Halliday, J and Soden, R (1998) Facilitating changes in lecturers' understanding of learning, *Teaching in Higher Education*, **3** (1), pp 21–35

Hannan, A and Silver, H (2000) *Innovating in Higher Education*, SRHE and Open University Press, Buckingham

Hewson, K and Paget, N (2001) Supervisor training in postgraduate medicine, *Focus on Health Professional Education*, **3** (1), pp 16–23

Hicks, O (1997) Career paths of directors of academic staff development units in Australian universities: the emergence of a species? *International Journal for Academic Development*, **2** (2), pp 56–63

Higgs, J and Edwards, H (eds) (1999) *Educating Beginning Practitioners: Challenges for health professional education*, Butterworth Heinemann, Oxford

Ho, A (1998) A conceptual change staff development programme: effects as perceived by participants, *International Journal for Academic Development*, **3** (1), pp 24–38

Ho, A (2000) A conceptual change approach to staff development: a model for programme design, *International Journal for Academic Development*, **5** (1), pp 30–41

Kahn, P and Baume, D (eds) (2003) *Understanding Educational Development*, Kogan Page, London

Kember, D (2000) *Action Learning and Action Research: Improving the quality of teaching and learning*, Kogan Page, London

Ketteridge, S, Marshall, S and Fry, H (2002) *The Effective Academic: A handbook for enhanced academic practice*, Kogan Page, London

Knapper, C (1998) Is academic development a profession? *International Journal for Academic Development*, **3** (2), pp 93–96

Knight, P (2002) *Being a Teacher in Higher Education*, SRHE and Open University Press, Buckingham

Kreber, C and Brook, P (2001) Impact evaluation of educational development programmes, *International Journal for Academic Development*, **6** (2), pp 96–108

Kugel, P (1993) How professors develop as teachers, *Studies in Higher Education*, **18** (3), pp 313–28

Laurillard, D (2002) *Rethinking University Teaching*, 2nd edn, Routledge, London

Leamnson, R (1999) *Thinking About Teaching and Learning*, Stylus, Sterling, VA

Macdonald, R and Wisdom, J (2002) *Academic and Educational Development: Research, evaluation and changing practice in higher education*, Kogan Page, London

Main, A (1985) *Educational Staff Development*, Croom Helm, London

Marshall, S, Fry, H and Ketteridge, S (eds) (1999) *A Handbook of Teaching and Learning in Higher Education: Enhancing academic practice*, Kogan Page, London

McAlpine, L and Harris, R (1999) Lessons learned: faculty developer and engineer working together as faculty development colleagues, *International Journal for Academic Development*, **4** (1), pp 11–17

Moon, J (1999) *Reflection in Learning and Professional Development: Theory and practice*, Kogan Page, London

Nicholls, G (2001) *Professional Development in Higher Education: New dimensions and directions*, Kogan Page, London

Nyquist, J (1996) *Working Effectively with Graduate Assistants*, Sage, Newbury Park

Panda, S (ed) (1997) *Staff Development in Higher and Distance Education*, Aravali Books International, New Delhi

Piccinin, S *et al* (1999) The impact of individual consultation on student ratings of teaching, *International Journal for Academic Development*, **4** (2), pp 75–88

Prosser, M and Trigwell, K (1998) *Understanding Learning and Teaching*, Open University Press, Buckingham

Rowland, S (2000) *The Enquiring University Teacher*, SRHE and Open University Press

Rowland, S *et al* (1998) Turning academics into teachers? *Teaching in Higher Education*, **3** (2), pp 133–41

Rust, C (1998) The impact of educational development workshops on teachers' practice, *International Journal for Academic Development*, **3** (1), pp 72–80

Schon, D (1987) *Educating the Reflective Practitioner*, Jossey-Bass, San Francisco

Squires, G (1999) *Teaching as a Professional Discipline*, Falmer Press, London

Stefani, L (1999) On becoming an academic developer: a personal journey, *International Journal for Academic Development*, **4** (2), pp 102–10

Walker, M (2001) *Reconstructing Professionalism in University Teaching: Teachers and learners in action*, SRHE and Open University Press, Buckingham

Webb, G (1996) Supporting academic development in departments, *International Journal for Academic Development*, **1** (1), pp 27–37

Webb, G (1996) *Understanding Staff Development*, SRHE and Open University Press, Buckingham

Web sites

Higher Education Research and Development Society of Australasia Inc (HERDSA) [accessed 21 January 2003] http://www.herdsa.org.au

Professional and Organizational Development in Higher Education (POD) [accessed 21 January 2003] http://www.podnetwork.org

Society for Research into Higher Education (SRHE) [accessed 21 January 2003] http://www.srhe.ac.uk

Society for Teaching and Learning in Higher Education (STLHE) [accessed 21 January 2003] http://www.tss.uoguelph.ca/stlhe

Staff and Educational Development Association (SEDA) [accessed 21 January 2003] http://www.seda.ac.uk

Index

Case Studies of Teaching in Higher Education Series

Assessment: Case Studies, Experience and Practice edited by Peter Schwartz and Graham Webb
0 7494 3689 1 (hardback)
0 7494 3623 9 (paperback)

Lecturing: Case Studies, Experience and Practice edited by Helen Edwards, Brenda Smith and Graham Webb
0 7494 3531 3 (hardback)
0 7494 3519 4 (paperback)

Online Learning and Teaching with Technology: Case Studies, Experience and Practice edited by David Murphy, Rob Walker and Graham Webb
0 7494 3529 1 (hardback)
0 7494 3520 8 (paperback)

Problem-Based Learning: Case Studies, Experience and Practice edited by Peter Schwartz, Stewart Mennin and Graham Webb
0 7494 3530 5 (hardback)
0 7494 3492 9 (paperback)

Supporting Student Learning: Case Studies, Experience and Practice edited by Glenda Crosling and Graham Webb
0 7494 3534 8 (hardback)
0 7494 3535 6 (paperback)

All titles are available from good bookshops. To obtain further information, please contact the publisher at the address below:

Kogan Page Ltd
120 Pentonville Road
London N1 9JN
Tel: 020 7278 0433
Fax: 020 7837 6348
www.kogan-page.co.uk